Marilyn

Marilyn

Kathy Rooks-Denes

Grange
BOOKS

A FRIEDMAN GROUP BOOK

Published by Grange Books
An imprint of Books & Toys Limited
The Grange
Grange Yard
London SE1 3AG

ISBN 1 85627 289 3

MARILYN
was prepared and produced by
Michael Friedman Publishing Group, Inc.
15 West 26th Street
New York, New York 10010

Editor: Elizabeth Viscott Sullivan
Art Director: Jeff Batzli
Designer: Susan Livingston
Photography Editor: Grace How

Colour separations by Rainbow Graphic Arts Co., Ltd.
Printed in Hong Kong and bound in China by Leefung-Asco Printers Ltd.

Grateful acknowledgement is given to authors, publishers, and
photographers for permission to reprint material. Every effort has
been made to determine copyright owners of photographs and
illustrations. In the case of any omissions, the Publishers will be
pleased to make suitable acknowledgements in future editions.

To my parents, who shaped my life with a tender and reliable love—the type that sadly eluded Norma Jeane, despite her desperate desire to attain it.

Contents

Introduction

June 1 marks the birthday of a child who would grow to be a legend, and that date is celebrated annually by legions of fans worldwide. But on that day in 1926, no one could have foreseen the impact that a newborn named Norma Jeane Mortensen ultimately would have on generations of people. No one then would have believed that she would transform herself into the ultraglamorous enigma Marilyn Monroe.

For her mother, twenty-four-year-old Gladys Pearl Monroe Baker Mortensen, there was little cause to celebrate, because her daughter was born into a home environment almost devoid of happiness: Gladys was increasingly becoming a prisoner to depression. To make matters worse, Norma Jeane's father had abandoned the family, and this—coupled with the mystery surrounding his very identity—would haunt the child, and later the woman, throughout her life.

Despite the myriad trials she faced from birth, Norma Jeane persisted and earned many triumphs. She dreamed of becoming an actress, and not only realized that dream, but became a legend worldwide. She became Marilyn Monroe.

To remain adored for decades after one's death is no small feat, and Marilyn Monroe achieved legendary status without being a world leader or life-saving scientist. She became ingrained in modern culture by virtue of her personality—a volatile combination of deprivation, desire, and dogged determination to beat her personal struggles and the odds against her. That explosive combination

A confident Marilyn in 1955, after she turned her back on Hollywood to form Marilyn Monroe Productions.

created an intense energy and light that both attracted people to her and drained her. Still, the enigma of Marilyn Monroe captivates the world, even thirty years after her light was snuffed out by drugs and despair on late August 4 or early August 5, 1962.

Mental health experts, dozens of biographers, and fascinated fans have strived, to little avail it seems, to better understand Marilyn Monroe's complex personality and her tragic demise. Armed

Marilyn's 1950 performances in **The Asphalt Jungle** *and* **All About Eve** *boosted her popularity and career.*

with the advantage of hindsight and little else, they have dissected, categorized, and imposed their own perceptions of her in hopes of building a complete picture from the puzzle pieces of her life. Rather than try to pigeonhole Marilyn Monroe based on psychological and sociological measures, perhaps some understanding will best be achieved by chronicling her life, beginning with her childhood, which tragically lacked the nurturing and sense of security that many children take for granted.

The following account is based on published biographies, including Marilyn's unfinished "autobiography"; tributes; remembrances by those who knew her; and the mountains of magazine and newspaper articles that continue to be written about her. Although many of these sources were meticulously researched by their authors, it is important to note that the details given of Marilyn's personal life often are inconsistent. The following account is gleaned from chronology recognized as accurate in most of these resources and from independent sources.

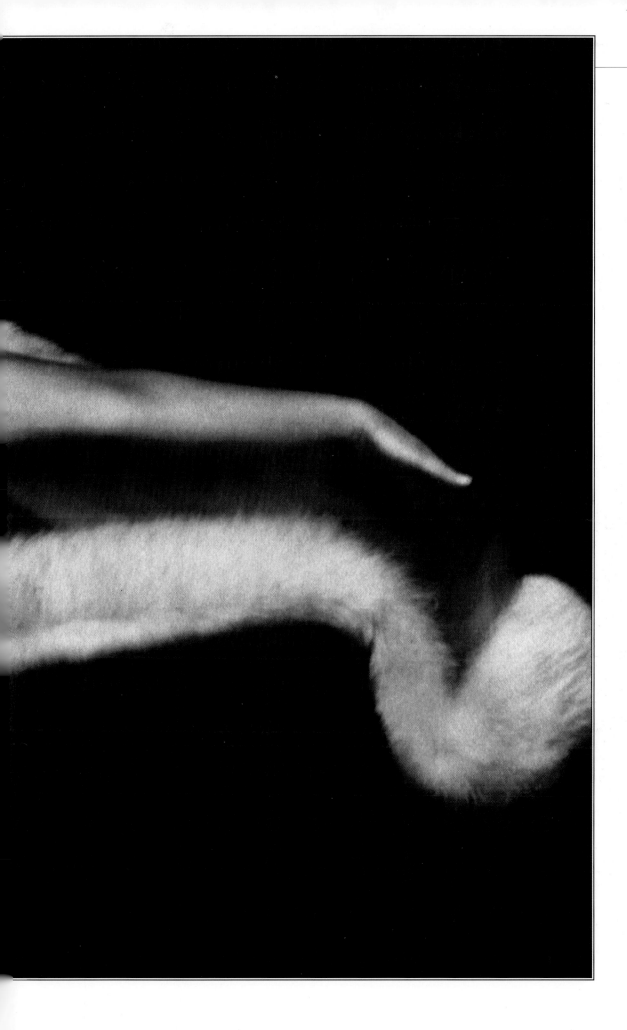

Marilyn once told a journalist that she wanted to become a character actor so that she could continue acting when she was no longer known for her sexuality. Citing Lee Strasberg, she said, "The art of the actor grows more rich with age, not less."

Chapter One

Norma Jeane

Being a movie actress

was never as much

fun as dreaming

of being one.

When Gladys Mortensen bore a fair-haired daughter she named Norma Jeane—after actress Norma Talmadge, who was then at the peak of her career—at 9:30 A.M. on June 1, 1926, at Los Angeles General Hospital (now County-USC Medical Center), she was divorced from her first husband and separated from her second, Ed Mortensen. Mortensen was listed as Norma Jeane's father on her birth certificate, but whether he was really her father remains a point of debate. The most popular speculation centers on C. Stanley Gifford, who met Gladys at Consolidated Film Industries, a Hollywood film-processing lab where he worked as a salesman, she as a film cutter. According to the adult Marilyn, who said she did not know until age five that her father might not be Mortensen, Gifford left Gladys on Christmas Eve 1925, when he learned she was pregnant.

Norma Jeane was not Gladys' only child. Gladys bore two children during her teenage marriage to Jack Baker (they wed in 1917, when Gladys was fifteen): a son, Hermitt Jack, and a daughter, Berneice. The two children were taken to live with their father's family in Kentucky when the Bakers divorced in 1921. Hermitt reportedly died of tuberculosis in the early 1920s, but Gladys listed both children as dead when Norma Jeane was born. (Berneice and Gladys were reunited in the mid-1960s, and Berneice became her mother's legal guardian in 1967.)

Once Norma Jeane was born, Gladys decided she couldn't keep both her job and a child; she could barely afford furnished rooms, and her medical bills were paid by coworkers who took up a collection at the film lab. Beginning June 12, she boarded Norma Jeane for about $25 a month with a mail carrier and his wife, Albert and Ida Bolender, who lived across from the Hawthorne, California, home of Gladys' mother, forty-nine-year-old Della Hogan Monroe Grainger. (Marilyn would later complain that families who took her in did so only for the $5 or so a week they received.)

Della had left Hawthorne before Norma Jeane was born, having rented out her own home so that she could join her second husband in India, where he had found an engineering job. In October, after just ten months in India, Della returned and began divorce proceedings against her husband. A few weeks later Della—formerly a devout follower of Sister Aimee Semple McPherson, leader of the Angelus Temple in Los Angeles—had her six-month-old granddaughter baptized as Norma Jeane Baker by Sister Aimee at the Foursquare Gospel Church in Hawthorne.

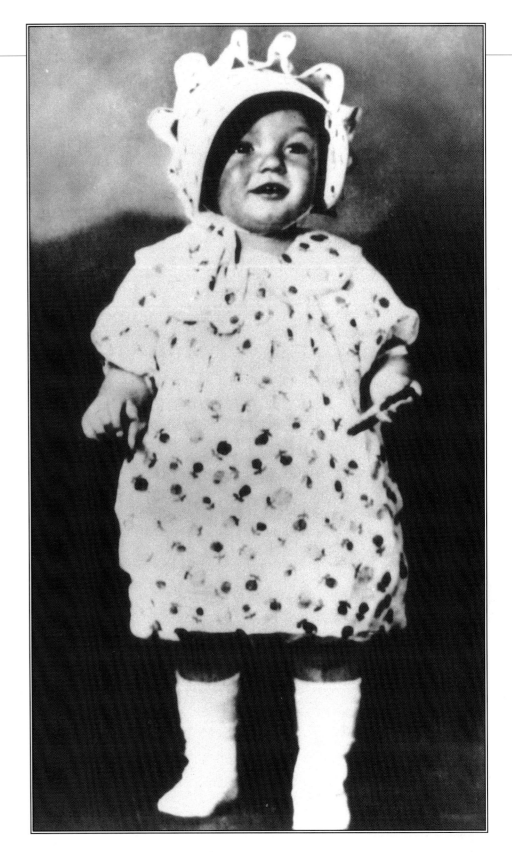

As a toddler, Norma Jeane lived with Albert and Ida Bolender, who were strict and devoutly religious. While not prone to displays of affection, they cared for their young charge enough to offer to adopt her.

Norma Jeane spent her first years with the Bolenders, a puritanical religious couple who boarded children at their two-acre (1ha) property and whose offers to adopt her were rejected by Gladys. The Bolenders were loving to the children but were strict disciplinarians; any infraction by their young boarders brought punishment by razor strop. But one misbehavior that brought Norma Jeane attention without stern punishment was exhibitionism, and so a strong desire to shed her clothes was instilled in her from childhood. Marilyn later revealed in her "autobiographical" *My Story* (the manuscript, supposedly written by Marilyn, was published twelve years after her death by Milton Greene) that this desire to be noticed did not stop at the Bolenders' door, but extended to another sort of sanctuary—church: "No sooner was I in the pew...than the impulse would come to me to take off all my clothes.... I wanted desperately to stand up naked for God and everyone else to see. I had to clench my teeth and sit on my hands to keep myself from undressing. Sometimes I had to pray hard and beg God to keep me from taking my clothes off.... My impulse to appear naked and my dreams about it had no shame or sense of sin in them. Dreaming of people looking at me made me feel less lonely."

Living across the street from her grandmother's home did not make life any easier for Norma Jeane, because when Della returned from India, she was on the verge of disaster herself. Once, Della rushed to the Bolenders' home to interrupt a razor-strop whipping that resulted when Norma Jeane threw her bowl of food on the floor, and she took the year-old toddler back to her home for a visit. Afterward, she would often bring the child to her house for visits. Marilyn would later insist that during one of these occasions she awoke from a nap in her grandmother's bedroom "fighting for my life. Something was pressed against my face. It could have been a pillow. I fought with all my strength." (Many biographers have downplayed this account, saying that Marilyn could not remember an incident that occurred when she was barely a year old.)

Marilyn on the set of her top-grossing film, **Some Like It Hot,** *in 1955. Her dress was so tight that she had to rest between takes in a custom-made chair that enabled her to "half-stand," allowing her to avoid wrinkling the garment.*

Another one of Della's "rescue" attempts occurred when she tried to break through the Bolenders' door—she had to be taken away by police. Della was placed in a Norwalk asylum on August 4, 1927, where she died less than three weeks later, on August 23, at age fifty-one, from an apparent heart attack during a manic seizure.

The complexity of young Norma Jeane's situation was not helped much even by the regular weekend visits from her mother. Norma Jeane remembered Gladys as "a pretty woman who never smiled" but never thought of her as "mama." In fact, she apparently did not know who Gladys really was until Ida Bolender pointed it out; she had called the Bolenders her mother and father, and Ida had corrected her. (Another child boarder near Norma Jeane's age, Lester, did get away with calling Ida Bolender "mama," because she and her husband had adopted the boy. Yet they referred to Norma Jeane and Lester as "the twins," which only added to the young girl's confusion.)

Gladys did pay for piano lessons for her daughter, and even left her new job as a film cutter at Columbia Pictures (a fire had closed Consolidated Film Industries) for three weeks to nurse Norma Jeane when she had whooping cough—the most intimate contact she'd had with her daughter. (Norma Jeane's recuperation also was aided by the affections of her dog, Tippy, which she'd been allowed to keep when it followed Albert Bolender home from work. She and the dog were inseparable—until it was shot to death by a neighbor who complained that the dog was constantly rolling about in his garden.) Gladys began to spend more time with her daughter, and she would bring Norma Jeane for occasional visits to her workplace and furnished room.

During one of these visits, five-year-old Norma Jeane was fascinated by a lone picture on her mother's wall of a handsome, dark-haired man sporting a mustache and cocked slouch hat. "That's your father," Gladys finally said as her daughter stared at the photograph. "I felt so excited

I almost fell off the chair," Marilyn recalled. "That was my first happy time." Gladys then told her he had been killed in an automobile accident, but young Norma Jeane didn't believe her.

The man in the photograph would be the object of hopeful fantasies for years to come, always showing up in Norma Jeane's imagination when she needed him, whether at her sickbed when she was hospitalized for a tonsillectomy or waiting for her at home on rainy days. But, Marilyn said, "I could never get him in my largest, deepest daydream to take off his hat

$\mathcal{M}$*arilyn's last completed film,* **The Misfits,** *finally brought her together with Clark Gable, with whom she had had a lifelong obsession.*

and sit down." And the resemblance of her "father" to Clark Gable would spark a lifelong obsession for the handsome actor, whom Norma Jeane sometimes would claim to classmates was her father.

This "happy time" for Norma Jeane would soon be followed by brighter days filled with hope. While Norma Jeane attended kindergarten with Lester at Ballona Elementary (later renamed Washington Elementary), Gladys worked double shifts to buy a small white bungalow in North Hollywood. Norma Jeane was brought to live with her mother in October 1934, along with an elderly English couple and their adult daughter (no biographers have been able to identify them by name), who helped take care of the child. Gladys even bought Norma Jeane a used white piano (Marilyn later would proudly point out that it had once belonged to actor Fredric March) and enrolled her at Selma Street School in Hollywood.

The English couple, both actors, encouraged little Norma to come out of the religious shell that the strict Bolenders had built around her. They taught her to juggle, dance, and sing. They introduced her to the silver screen at the nearby Grauman's Chinese and Egyptian theaters, where she would find solace and escape throughout her childhood and into her teens. For just 10¢ admission, Norma Jeane would watch movies for hours, sometimes forgetting to go home for dinner. But the well-spoken couple— especially the man, who worked regularly as a stand-in for the oh-so-proper actor George Arliss— also insisted that she use correct English. With her vocabulary of "ain'ts" and "don't gots" from life with the less sophisticated Bolenders, who were both from rural areas, Norma Jeane became hesitant to speak for fear of saying the wrong thing. In the process of her instruction, however, English became her strongest subject at school.

Gladys continued to work double shifts to pay the bills and was renting most of the house to the English couple, but her attempt to provide her daughter a home and family life was short-lived. In January 1935, Gladys called the film lab to say she couldn't come to work. Marilyn later recounted how she and the renters heard a loud noise in the stairway, and how her mother, hiding in the staircase, had to be forcibly removed, strapped to a stretcher. (Accounts by biographers insist Norma Jeane was actually at school when her mother was taken away.) Gladys was taken to the hospital where Norma Jeane had been born, then transported to the same Norwalk mental center in which her mother, Della, had died five years earlier. Gladys was diagnosed with paranoid schizophrenia, an illness that had destroyed both her parents and her older brother; she would remain institutionalized almost all her life.

Following Gladys' breakdown, Norma Jeane remained with the English couple for about a year, but during the first two months of that period, the actors lost the house; they were eventually forced to move back to England due to lack of work. While the couple was struggling to stay in

Because she was frequently relocated, the details of Norma Jeane's life from the time of her mother's nervous breakdown in 1935 until the end of her tenure in the orphanage in 1937 are sketchy. Despite researchers' valiant attempts to chronicle Norma Jeane's early years, firm facts of much of this period are nonexistent. Sometime during that period she lived with a couple named Sam and Enid Knebelcamp—they were the only former foster parents to attend Marilyn's 1962 funeral. Even as an adult, Marilyn had trouble recalling where she was at what time and with which foster family—as any person would. Childhood memories are diluted by youth, the passage of time, and confusion between fantasy and fact.

Marilyn repeatedly claimed that during a stay in one of her many foster homes, she was molested at age eight by an older boarder, a man she identified as "Mr. Kimmel." She said he called her into his room, then

No one ever told me I was pretty when I was a little girl. All little girls should be told they're pretty, even if they aren't.

the bungalow and later living in furnished rooms, Grace McKee, Gladys' closest friend from Columbia Pictures, helped pay Norma Jeane's expenses with money provided by the studio; it was at this time that she began her role as a fairly steady presence in the young girl's life.

Grace was named Norma Jeane's guardian by county authorities, and after the English couple left, she quickly found another family to take the girl in. That couple, Harvey Giffen and his wife, had been neighbors of Gladys and Norma Jeane when mother and daughter shared the Hollywood bungalow, and they were very fond of the young girl. But when the Giffens planned to return to their home state of Mississippi and wanted to adopt Norma Jeane so that she could remain with them and their three children, Gladys refused. She also refused an adoption offer from a friend from her days at Consolidated, Reginald Carroll, and his wife. So despite at least three attempts to adopt her and the fact that her mother was still alive, Norma Jeane spent her childhood with twelve different families, ten of them foster families, when she wasn't in a Los Angeles orphanage.

locked the door and molested her while she quietly fought him. "He said, 'It's only a game'; he let me go when the game was over," Marilyn said. When Norma Jeane left the room, she stammered to her foster mother what had happened but was not believed. "I cried… all night," she said. "I just wanted to die." Apparently few people believed her story, even when she recounted it frequently as an adult. However, the stammer that she said first surfaced at that time would recur whenever she was nervous or criticized, leading her to assume her trademark breathless tone as a remedy when she became a starlet.

As "Aunt" Grace McKee took more and more interest in Norma Jeane, the child came to view her as her best friend. Grace "was the first person who ever patted my head or touched my cheek," Marilyn wrote. "That happened when I was 8. I can still remember how thrilled I felt when her kind hand touched me." But Grace's concern for Gladys' daughter was not enough to provide the child with a stable environment. Norma Jeane would stay with Aunt Grace occasionally, but when Grace planned to be married to Erwin "Doc" Goddard, a divorced man ten years her junior with three children of his own, "the house became too small, and someone had to go," Marilyn recalled.

On September 13, 1935, nine-year-old Norma Jeane was driven by Grace to the Los Angeles Orphans Home Society (now called Hollygrove), a Hollywood orphanage that would be her home for the next two years. (Noted Monroe biographer Fred Guiles, in his 1969 book *Norma Jean*, says the Goddards were not wed until after Norma Jeane left the orphanage two years later.) "I saw this sign, and the emptiness that came over me, I'll never forget," said Marilyn during the last summer of her life to photographer George Barris, who authored the 1986 biography *Marilyn* with Gloria Steinem. "I still remember they had to drag me inside that place.... The whole world around me just crumbled." But Grace, who was making barely enough money to support herself, did leave Norma Jeane with the promise to take her out of the orphanage as soon as she possibly could.

Norma Jeane's experience in the orphanage was not all negative. During her first Christmas there, nearby RKO Studios invited the orphanage children to visit its facilities, treating them to candy, ice cream, and a movie. She also discovered the wonders of makeup, courtesy of the orphanage director, and reportedly was an outstanding athlete on the orphanage softball team. "When I look back on those days I remember, in fact, that they were full of all sorts of fun and excitement," Marilyn wrote. "I played games in the sun and ran races. I also had daydreams, not only about my father's photograph but about many other things. I daydreamed chiefly about beauty." And the beauty she so desperately desired soon would begin to take form, following the lead of her quickly developing body. She said that at age ten she shot up to her adult height of five-foot-five (162.5cm),

Norma Jeane in 1945, six months after being discovered by Army photographer David Conover.

This innocent pigtails-and-pinafore look in 1945 soon gave way to the cheese-cake poses that comprised the majority of Norma Jeane's modeling assignments.

would take Norma Jeane with them to make deliveries, prompting her to complain to Grace that she spent all her time in their battered car. Grace then found the girl another home with a couple who took in "county children," but the father was an alcoholic, so in the end Grace brought Norma Jeane into her home in West Van Nuys in early 1938 for an extended stay. There, Norma Jeane finally had her own bedroom, until Grace's stepdaughter, Beebe, who was two years younger, moved back in with the Goddards after a year of living with her own mother.

At age eleven, Norma Jeane enrolled at Lankershim (elementary) School in North Hollywood, then attended grades seven through nine at Emerson Junior High School, a term behind others her age because of her frequent moves. It was in junior high school that she discovered what it meant to have a body more mature than her years. "When I was 12 years old I may have still been a baby inside, but outside I had the body of a woman," Marilyn wrote. Her rapid physical progress brought her more attention than she had ever had—boys swarmed around her, and girls often glared at her in envy—but she was uncomfortable when she was pursued sexually. "I used to lie awake at night wondering why the boys came after me," Marilyn wrote. "I didn't want them that way. I wanted to play games in the street, not in the bedroom. Occasionally I let one of them kiss me to see if there was anything in the performance. There wasn't. I finally decided that the boys came after me because I was an orphan and had no parents to protect me or frighten them off. This decision made me cooler than ever."

The boys clamored to walk her home from school, but Norma Jeane remained shy and socially reserved (she was so timid that the Goddards called her "Mouse"). Her years in foster homes had taught her that silence and keeping a low profile were critical to avoid being sent back to the orphanage "in shame."

As a thirteen-year-old, Marilyn said, she realized she was a "siren," but had no idea why: "There were no thoughts of sex in my head. I didn't want to be kissed." Still, she relished the attention she had so long craved;

prompting her classmates to call her "String Bean" and "The Human Bean," and what she called her "precocious curves" began to be evident well before those of her peers.

In June 1937, Norma Jeane moved in with a Compton couple, an arrangement maneuvered by Grace to fulfill her promise to get Norma Jeane out of the orphanage after she and another girl were caught trying to run away. The couple ran a furniture-polish business out of their home and nurtured by her physical attractiveness, she began to develop a previously unknown attitude of self-assurance over the next couple years. However, her maturing body also brought her intense pain in the form of menstrual cramps. These cramps and other gynecological complications plagued her for her entire life, and are pointed to by many as a factor in establishing her dependence on pills. Norma Jeane was unblemished by the facial calamities that befall most teenagers (she sometimes would wash her face more than a dozen times a day), and Grace gave her home permanents to make her straight hair stylishly curly. But aside from the attention her looks brought, Norma Jeane found another form of attention, a motherly love that had been so long denied her, when she was befriended by Grace's aunt, Ana Lower.

Norma Jeane spent every Sunday with Ana, a devout Christian Scientist who had never married and had no children. Ana advised Grace to give Norma Jeane chores that differed from those she had had at the orphanage, to keep her from being reminded of those years. The girl attended church regularly with her "aunt," whom Marilyn called "the greatest influence on my whole life." Norma Jeane eventually moved in with "Aunt" Ana after the following incident at the Goddard house.

The Goddards had moved into Ana's Van Nuys ranch home, and Ana had bought a two-story house in West Los Angeles, renting out the bottom floor. Norma Jeane had her own bedroom in the ranch house and liked living there simply because it had belonged to Ana. It was there that Grace's husband, Doc, whom Norma Jeane now called "Daddy," barged into the fourteen-year-old girl's bedroom one evening early in 1941, apparently very drunk, and kissed her intimately. He expressed regret about the incident when he sobered up, but when Norma Jeane told Ana what had happened, she invited the girl to

With her husband away in the Merchant Marine, Norma Jeane rolled up her sleeves to pursue modeling with a vengeance.

Photographers appreciated Norma Jeane's natural look. Her instinctive performance for the camera rendered almost every shot usable.

move in with her. (Norma Jeane's relationship with
Goddard supposedly remained normal thereafter, and
he served as her first business manager when her acting career began to take off more than five years later.)

At age fifteen Norma Jeane transferred from Van
Nuys High School to University High School in West
Los Angeles and enjoyed a close relationship with her
Aunt Ana. The happiness she found with Ana would
last barely more than a year, for Doc Goddard soon was
told by his employer, Adel Precision Products, that he
would be promoted, but the promotion was contingent
on his moving to West Virginia. Grace encouraged him
to accept; they made plans to move, and those plans
did not include taking Norma Jeane with them. Ana, in
her early sixties, apparently was considered too old to
be the girl's legal guardian. Grace decided marriage
would be the best alternative for the teen, as the other
choices were rather grim: more years in the orphanage
or foster care.

Grace quickly arranged a marriage of conve-
nience between Norma Jeane and Jim Dougherty, the
twenty-year-old son of Grace's neighbors. Dougherty
was a star football player in high school who had passed
up college to work two jobs after growing up in
Depression-era poverty. He was a casual acquaintance
and sometime suitor of his future bride, although
Norma Jeane had always thought he was more interested in Beebe than in her. Dougherty often drove the
two girls home after school.

Despite protests by Norma Jeane that she was too
young to marry, the two began a courtship and were wed
eighteen days after her sixteenth birthday. "You know,
I had six mothers weeping when I marched down the aisle," Marilyn said.
"They were all my foster mothers." The Bolenders attended the ceremony,
but the Goddards were absent. Gladys was absent as well; although
released from Norwalk hospital a year earlier, she had suffered a relapse
after moving to San Francisco and was hospitalized in that area.

Jim Dougherty and sixteen-year-old Norma Jeane on their wedding day, June 19, 1942.

Norma Jeane became Mrs. Jim Dougherty at the Westwood home of Chester Howell, a friend of the Dougherty family, in a white dress provided by her beloved Aunt Ana, who also gave her away. There was little real emotion to speak of—unless one includes Dougherty's annoyance at Norma Jeane's enthusiasm for champagne and dancing during their Florentine Gardens restaurant reception—and no honeymoon. On Monday morning, Dougherty returned to his job at Lockheed, an aviation plant, and Norma Jeane went about getting their new one-room Sherman Oaks apartment in order. The couple spent their weekends engaging in outdoor activities (such as fishing) or attending entertainment outings, and they went to church on Sunday mornings.

Although the Doughertys seemed happy enough, Marilyn later wrote of that 1942 union: "It was like being retired to a zoo. The first effect marriage had on me was to increase my lack of interest in sex…. Actually our marriage was a sort of friendship with sexual privileges, [which] brought me neither happiness nor pain." The greatest benefit of the marriage, Marilyn said, was that it finally ended her status as an "orphan." "I felt grateful to Jim for this," she said.

Marilyn was an avid reader. She always brought books with her on the set, often reading between takes.

But the marriage also meant the end of her formal education, because she dropped out of high school, never to return. She spent the rest of her life trying to compensate for her lack of "book" knowledge.

Norma Jeane filled the first two years of her stint as Mrs. Dougherty with domestic pursuits. While Dougherty worked at Lockheed, he said, she kept their home spotless—first the tiny apartment, then a larger house in Van Nuys, and finally the former home of his parents and brother, who had moved into a larger residence in North Hollywood. Dougherty wanted his wife to stay at home, so Norma Jeane's penchant for tidiness may have been more a consequence of intense boredom than true pride in house-keeping. She also tried to learn to cook, but without as much success. Possibly her greatest kitchen triumph was her discovery that carrots and peas made an eye-pleasing color combination on the plate, Dougherty said.

Norma Jeane packed Dougherty's lunch every day and usually added a love note. Dougherty said that despite the lack of interest in sex she later expressed as Marilyn regarding her adolescence and first marriage, Norma

Jeane was not only accommodating in the physical aspects of their four-year union, but was often the initiator. He added that Norma Jeane was desperate in the early stages of their marriage to have a child, but he talked her out of it, buying her a collie for companionship instead. She also began to be obsessed with tracking down her father.

In late 1943, Dougherty joined the Merchant Marine as an instructor in physical training on Santa Catalina Island. There, Norma Jeane took up weight lifting under the guidance of former Olympic champion Howard Carrington and spent the evenings dancing, often with her husband watching from the sidelines. She and Dougherty fished, swam, and enjoyed each other's company on the island, growing closer in their relative seclusion (Dougherty says that Norma Jeane once said she would jump off the pier if he ever left her). Dougherty would rush home each day after work to be with his young wife. But in 1944, life changed drastically when Dougherty got his orders to go to Australia and the Far East.

According to Dougherty, Norma Jeane was overwhelmed by the prospect of again being left alone and frantically begged him to make her pregnant "so that she could have a piece of me, in case something happened." But it was not to be. (Marilyn disputed wanting children at this point, saying she didn't want a daughter who would grow up, like her, without a father.) About this time, Dougherty said, eighteen-year-old Norma Jeane announced she was going to call her father. He watched her dial a number and quickly hang up, saying the man had refused to talk to her. Similar scenes would be repeated in years to come in front of many different people.

When her husband left, Norma Jeane packed up their belongings and moved in with the Dougherty family in North Hollywood. Her mother-in-law, Ethel, was a comforting presence, but Norma Jeane could not sustain for long the wifely role expected of her. She joined Ethel Dougherty as an employee at Radio Plane Company, the Burbank plant that produced targets for military exercises. Norma Jeane began as a parachute inspector and was then promoted to the "dope room," where she sprayed liquid dope (a mix of banana oil and glue) on plane fuselages. But hardworking Norma Jeane's life was about to assume a drastically different course from that of her blue-collar colleagues, almost all of whom were women and almost all of whom were fairly cool toward her.

David Conover, a photographer under the command of Captain Ronald Reagan at the Army's pictorial center in Hollywood, walked through the Radio Plane plant in late June 1945 in search of subjects for

Early poses, such as this one in 1946, featured Norma Jeane's natural smile, which she soon was advised to modify by lowering her lip to achieve a more glamorous look.

Norma Jeane accompanied photographer Andre de Dienes on a photo shoot across the northwestern United States in December 1945. Soon after this photograph was taken, they visited her mother, who had just been released from a hospital in Portland, Oregon. Norma Jeane brought her a scarf, perfume, and chocolates, but "they had nothing to say to each other," de Dienes recalled.

his camera, and an attractive young woman in overalls caught his eye. Conover told Norma Jeane, "I'm going to take your picture for the boys in the Army to keep their morale high." He then persuaded her to change into the tight sweater she kept in her locker.

Taken over a three-day period, those photographs marked the beginning of a new life for Norma Jeane and gave her, for the first time, some control over her future.

The photographs were published in *Yank* and *Stars and Stripes* magazines. Conover also showed the pictures to a commercial photographer in Los Angeles, Potter Hueth, who was impressed by Norma Jeane's "natural look." Hueth offered her the chance to pose for additional photographs under an agreement whereby she would be paid when he sold them for publication; this usually amounted to about $5 or $10 per photograph for Norma Jeane, who later remembered the seemingly small sum as "a lot of money in those days."

But Hueth's major contribution to the aspiring model's career was to show some of those photographs to Emmeline Snively, who ran the largest modeling agency in Los Angeles, the Blue Book Model Agency, as well as a modeling school. She saw potential in Norma Jeane's smiling features and well-developed curves, said she believed her talents were being wasted at the defense plant, and invited her to enroll in her modeling school. When Norma Jeane met with Snively on Monday, August 2, 1945, at her Ambassador Hotel office, she told the modeling agent she could not afford the Blue Book school's $100 tuition. Snively said she would allow her to pay it off over time with money she would earn from modeling assignments. Norma Jeane did not, however, tell Snively that she was married.

Later that day, Norma Jeane landed her first modeling job, a ten-day stint as hostess for Holga Steel Company's aluminum exhibit at the Los Angeles Home Show. The $10 she earned per day, plus the "sick leave"

Right: Norma Jeane's wedding portrait.
Below: Another early modeling shot.

pay she was receiving while playing hooky from Radio Plane, made it easy for Norma Jeane to pay off her modeling-school tuition. She was exhilarated by the potential for future earnings and by the chance for attention her new career brought her.

At first Norma Jeane wrote often to her faraway husband, professing how she loved and missed him, but then her letters subsided and took on a different tone, mostly describing her newfound vocation. Dougherty's initial response was tolerance, as he had become accustomed to the unpredictable when it came to his young wife. Meanwhile, Norma Jeane continued her eight-hour day shifts at the plant and attended modeling classes in the evenings. According to author Fred Guiles, with Dougherty too far away to be much affected by her harried schedule, the only victim of her neglect during this period was her pet collie, Muggsie, who died a year later—supposedly of "a broken heart"—when Norma Jeane left the pet with the Doughertys and returned to Ana Lower's home to live.

With her second modeling assignment came a different kind of attention; in Marilyn's words, the job "turned out quite bad." She and a group of

Norma Jeane caused quite a stir when she donned swimwear for the cameras.

models were on location at a Malibu beach to pose in a line of sports clothes for a Montgomery Ward catalog. "After two days they sent me home," she recalled. "They wouldn't tell me why, and I was upset—here I was, the only model fired." She later found out that she was dismissed because of her curvaceous figure, which, it was feared, would bring more attention than the clothing. So Snively, concluding that Norma Jeane had "more than the usual amount of sex appeal," started directing her toward nonfashion assignments, that is, those that generally involved bathing suits. "All of a sudden I became popular," Marilyn said. She was featured on a few magazine covers and Earl Moran calendars, which gave her the confidence to quit her job at Radio Plane.

Beyond becoming recognized for her figure, Norma Jeane became a model whom photographers found easy to work with. She not only took direction well, she often went beyond any need for supervision. Norma Jeane had finally found a relationship over which she had almost total control; she had a love affair with the camera that held even established photographers in awe. She may have had little or no working knowledge of lighting or the mechanics of film, but she controlled her features and expressions so well that some photographers said her modeling prowess made every shot usable.

At Snively's insistence, Norma Jeane finally had her light brown hair bleached to help her get more modeling jobs. She resisted until a much-needed shampoo assignment hinged on her being a blonde. "I couldn't get used to myself, but it did bring me more modeling work," Marilyn said. "I was getting more and more assignments for glamour poses and cheese-cake." Snively also instructed her to alter her smile, saying one photographer had decided Norma Jeane's nose looked too long because of the shadow it cast. "Try smiling with your upper lip drawn down," Snively told her, explaining this would compensate for not having "enough upper lip between the end of your nose and your mouth." The quiver that resulted when Norma Jeane tried to lower the upper part of her smile would never totally disappear, and this quiver would join her breathless speech and distinctive wiggle walk as part of her unique style.

Photographer Eve Arnold, author of the 1987 book *Marilyn Monroe—An Appreciation*, said that Norma Jeane's modeling skills were more than instinctive, that she would scrutinize the carefully controlled shots featured in movie magazines, learning from those and from every

What was to become the "Marilyn" look was born when Norma Jeane dyed her hair blonde for a shampoo commercial.

Cheesecake poses made Norma Jeane quite popular with the troops—and, according to Hollywood lore, with studio mogul Howard Hughes.

Merchant Marine as World War II drew to a close, Dougherty decided to resign his job and come home to Norma Jeane. But he was considered too valuable in his position, and the discharge request was denied.

By the end of 1945, Dougherty came home on leave for the Christmas holidays and was determined to stay closer to his wife by taking only West Coast voyages. He said he and Norma Jeane enjoyed a "marathon sexual reunion" at a San Fernando Valley motor lodge, but soon afterward Norma Jeane's loyalty to her modeling pursuits became painfully clear. Dougherty was now the one frantic to have children; Norma Jeane refused, saying she did not want to risk losing her figure. Dougherty discouraged her ambitions, but that made her all the more determined to achieve them. Rather than stay home that December with her husband, nineteen-year-old Norma Jeane opted to accompany thirty-two-year-old New York photographer Andre de Dienes, immigrant son of a Hungarian banker, for photo sessions across the northwestern states.

On that trip, de Dienes said, Norma Jeane staunchly refused his numerous requests that she pose in the nude and rebuffed the smitten photographer's advances—until, he said, they were forced to share a hotel room when no other was available, and she finally relented to lovemaking. De Dienes further claimed that when they returned to Los Angeles, he asked her to marry him, and she accepted. He said he later sent her money to finance her divorce from Dougherty, but was told over the telephone that the affair was off, just before he was to drive to Las Vegas to marry her. Dougherty, for his part, remembered Norma Jeane calling him often during her trip, sometimes in tears, saying she wished she had stayed home with him. De Dienes also recalled that his model often was distressed, but he said she was upset about causing him to lose his camera equipment by leaving the car unlocked and about an awkward visit with her mother in Portland, Oregon.

Norma Jeane's indiscretion, although unknown to Dougherty and denied by her for many years, may have served to further the gap between

photo session. Arnold, who first met Marilyn in the early 1950s, wrote: "Although her early stills are highly derivative, she was smart enough and skilled enough to find her own style. She was the master of the still camera—she was the animal trainer and the photographer was the beast. Being photographed was being caressed and appreciated in a very safe way."

With her husband overseas, Norma Jeane pursued modeling with a vengeance. But her developing love affair with the camera didn't stop at the still variety; she was becoming determined to pursue a career in front of the movie cameras as well. She was convinced that the exposure from her modeling jobs would help her get the break she needed to start an acting career, and her ambition worried her husband. Still overseas with the her and her frequently absent husband, but her modeling career and hopes for a break into films apparently were the deciding factors in their impending breakup. But before Dougherty left, for the last time as her husband, two other people reentered Norma Jeane's life: her mother, Gladys, and Grace Goddard.

In early 1946, just before Dougherty had to return to his ship duties, Gladys decided to try life outside of the mental hospital. While in the institution, she had become a devout Christian Scientist and had found some new strength in the religion's philosophies. Grace Goddard had recently returned to Los Angeles, and Gladys stayed with the Goddards until she and Norma Jeane moved into a vacated apartment downstairs from Ana

Norma Jeane justified missing meals by thinking how much good it did her career to have a washboard stomach. She worked out with weights so she could firmly carry her curves and was one of the first people to swear by the benefits of running. She also used "the sort of instinct that leads a duck to water" to continue finding jobs at photographers' studios. Despite her successes, she still felt somewhat empty: "I looked at the streets with lonely eyes. I had no relatives…or chums…. I had only myself."

Norma Jeane's shyness kept her from striking up many friendships, but it didn't keep her from leaving her Hollywood room to join the outside world. When not looking for work on the weekend, she would stroll the sidewalks with no particular destination in mind, ignoring the "wolves" on

T'm so many people. They shock me sometimes. I wish I was just me. I used to think I was going crazy, until I discovered some people I admired were like that too.

Lower. After living almost all her life as an "orphan" in the homes of families to which she could never belong, Norma Jeane at last seemed to be finding a family of her own.

Norma Jeane's life with her mother was never easy, but she, Gladys, and Aunt Ana spent each Sunday together, attending Christian Science services. After a few months, however, Norma Jeane left the others behind, and to bolster her modeling career and help her realize her acting ambitions, moved into Studio Club, a rooming house for starlets. (Gladys remained in the outside world only seven months before her depression again took hold and she asked to be readmitted to the hospital.)

Norma Jeane continued to make the rounds at photographers' studios, driving Dougherty's five-year-old Ford in search of work. She also often went on her job hunts on an empty stomach. "It didn't matter, though," Marilyn wrote. "When you're young and healthy a little hunger isn't too important." Although she was persistent enough to find a great many modeling jobs, much of the work she found was for photographers who were just as desperate for employment as she was and, in some cases, almost as broke. She refused to turn to Grace and Ana for help. "I knew how they needed the half-dollars in their purses, so I stayed away unless I had money and could take them to a restaurant or the movies."

the sidewalk who would proposition her as she passed by. A favorite spot to frequent on Sundays was Union Station, where she would watch the crowds for hours.

Occasionally someone would strike up a conversation with Norma Jeane and find in her an eager listener. One such person that Marilyn would remember later in her memoirs was Bill Cox, a nearly eighty-year-old veteran whom she met as they walked out of a restaurant together. He invited her to his home to meet his wife, and Norma Jeane became a regular visitor. The two would take walks and Cox would talk, "chiefly about the Spanish-American War in which he had been a soldier and about Abraham Lincoln," whom Marilyn had admired since she was a young girl. When his health began to deteriorate, Cox moved back to his home state of Texas with his wife. Norma Jeane would answer letters from the Coxes, but when his wife finally wrote that Cox had died, the streets only became "lonelier than ever."

Somehow, this loneliness seemed to propel her toward realizing her dreams: "I used to think as I looked out on the Hollywood night, 'There must be thousands of girls sitting alone like me dreaming of becoming a movie star. But I'm not going to worry about them. I'm dreaming the hardest.'" She also may have been working the hardest.

"Things were really happening for me as a model," Marilyn wrote. In the spring of 1946 she had made her cover premiere, gracing the front of *Family Circle* magazine dressed in a pinafore and holding a lamb. Her "cheesecake" poses, photographs in which she was usually clad in a bathing suit or shorts and halter top, were frequent features in the men's magazines of the day such as *Swank*, *Sir*, *Peek*, *Titter*, and *Laff*—very tame publications by modern standards. She was relishing her independence and planning to end her marriage to Dougherty, who again was on a long voyage, this time to China. (In fact, it was in China, after shopping for gifts for Norma Jeane, that Dougherty received the divorce papers from her lawyer on July 5. Dougherty decided not to sign the documents until he could meet with his wife face to face.)

In order to be able to attain a quick Nevada divorce, Norma Jeane went to Las Vegas to fulfill the six-week residency requirement there. The highlight of her Las Vegas tenure was meeting Roy Rogers and his film crew, who were there on location for filming, and riding Rogers' horse, Trigger. (Also at this time, Norma Jeane had to endure a case of trench mouth, which she had treated at Las Vegas General Hospital.)

Regarding the divorce, Norma Jeane's correspondence to Snively indicated that she wanted to remain friendly with her estranged husband. She wanted to cut the ties with her past to further her career, but she didn't want to hurt the man who had shown her so much regard as his wife. She said, "When my lawyer wrote to Jim in Shanghai about my wanting a divorce, Jim asked if I would wait until he returned from overseas to see if we could make a go of our marriage. It was then that I knew more than ever I wanted to become an actress." Coincidentally, her aspirations were on the way to being realized shortly after she decided to end her marriage.

The publicized story is that Norma Jeane's big break came when Howard Hughes, then owner of RKO Studios, saw her picture on the cover of one of the men's magazines he had pored over during a hospital stay after a flying accident and directed his studio to do a screen test for her. This account—told to Hollywood columnists Hedda Hopper and Louella Parsons by Emmeline Snively, who later admitted fabricating the story— appeared in *The Los Angeles Times* in July 1946 and attracted the attention of Ben Lyon, a talent scout at Twentieth Century-Fox.

Lyon, saying that Hughes' interest in Norma Jeane was enough to justify his seeing her, put off arranging a screen test for the novice actress

Newly signed starlet "Marilyn Monroe" soon discovered that "in Hollywood, a girl's virtue is much less important than her hairdo."

(her only acting experience to date had been in high school plays, where she usually played male roles). Lyon's excuse was that studio head Darryl Zanuck was out of town for some time, and that any color screen tests had to be approved by Zanuck. But Harry Lipton, a representative of Helen Ainsworth's talent agency who was hired to further Norma Jeane's career, threatened to take his client to RKO Studios instead. Lyon finally relented.

Norma Jeane's screen test was shot by cameraman Leon Shamroy, who, according to her, was "the best." When Shamroy disapproved of her makeup, he introduced her to Allan "Whitey" Snyder, who would become her favorite makeup artist and lifelong close friend. The test took place at dawn on July 19 on the set of a Betty Grable picture in production called *Mother Wore Tights*. According to Marilyn, the trio sneaked onto the set and procured an evening gown out of wardrobe for Norma Jeane. Then, with Shamroy doing all the lighting and camera loading, she was directed to walk across the stage, sit down, light a cigarette and put it out, go upstage, cross, look out the window, sit down, come downstage, and then exit.

"Those bright lights were blinding," Marilyn remembered. "For some strange reason, instead of being nervous and scared, I just tried very hard because I knew Mr. Lyon and Mr. Shamroy were taking an awful chance. If it didn't work out well, they might get into trouble."

Although she didn't say a word, Norma Jeane spoke volumes in front of the camera. Shamroy raved about the sexuality she exuded. By the time she left the sound stage, her one goal—to become an actress—was within reach. The footage of the test was shown to Zanuck that week, and he hired her for a six-month trial at a salary of $75 a week.

With the approach of autumn 1946, Jim Dougherty delivered his divorce documents to Norma Jeane's residence. He was met at the door by

By autumn 1946, "Norma Jeane" was pushed aside by a new look, a new studio contract, and a new name.

a "radiant" young starlet, who told him that earlier in the week she had secured a contract as a stock player at Twentieth Century-Fox. (Because of her orphan status, and because she was still under the age of twenty-one, her guardian, Grace Goddard, had been required to sign her contract.) As Dougherty made official the end of Norma Jeane's four-year tenure as Mrs. Dougherty, she also told him she had a new name: Marilyn Monroe. "Marilyn," Ben Lyon's suggestion, was after Marilyn Miller, an actress of 1920s musicals fame; Monroe was the maiden name of Norma Jeane's mother and deemed a perfect complement to the sound of "Marilyn."

"This is the end of my story of Norma Jeane," Marilyn wrote many years later. But she continued: "When I just wrote 'this is the end of Norma Jeane,' I blushed as if I had been caught in a lie. Because this sad, bitter child who grew up too fast is hardly ever out of my heart. With success all around me, I can still feel her frightened eyes looking out of mine. She keeps saying, 'I never lived, I was never loved,' and often I get confused and think it's I who am saying it."

Chapter Two

The Rocky Road to Fame

I'd like to be a fine actress.

Acting is my life. As far as

I'm concerned, the happiest

time is now. There's

a future and I

can't wait to get to it.

By autumn 1946, Norma Jeane was a starlet who was trying to get used to calling herself Marilyn Monroe. But the truth was, Marilyn was still little more than a model. At the time of her signing, the studios seemed to have more starlets than they could use. Their philosophy for success during that period was to spend their way out of financial trouble, and they often went to great expense to train and publicize those under contract.

Although Marilyn had a contract and a weekly paycheck, she had no roles. She spent her time taking classes in acting, pantomime, singing, and dancing. She recited scripts on deserted soundstages. She went to studio screenings to watch other actresses work. She posed for "endless still pictures" and rode in parades. Once while participating in one of those many pageants, the starlet was asked for her autograph; to this request she shyly asked, "How do you spell Marilyn Monroe?"

Marilyn's first spoken lines to survive editing-room cuts can be heard in the 1947 release **Dangerous Years,** *in which she played a waitress.*

But Marilyn was beginning to enjoy her independence and life as a single woman, even before her divorce was finalized. Whatever revulsion she might have claimed to have had toward libidinous males during her teens was now outweighed at times by her need for companionship, adventure, and advancement. So began a long string of relationships and affairs that would prove fascinating gossip fodder during her lifetime and well beyond.

Among those of her early beaus who published accounts about their relationship was Robert Slatzer, a budding magazine writer from Ohio who was nineteen when Norma Jeane literally stumbled into his life in mid-1946. Slatzer met her before she became a starlet and changed her name. He happened to be watching one day when she tripped in through the front door of the Twentieth Century-Fox studio building, strewing her photo-filled modeling portfolio across the floor in the process. Slatzer described the scene as follows: "I went to her rescue, and I'm glad to say there was only one place for her to sit down and wait—next to me. She said her name was Norma Jeane Mortensen…. We ended up making a date for that very same evening."

Slatzer was among the many suitors she would have during that summer as she waited for her divorce decree. Slatzer claims that he and Marilyn were married six years later in Mexico, but that she had the marriage terminated after just three days due to the insistence of her studio.

Another chance meeting in the studio's administration building during the first year of her contract would prove much more beneficial, at least careerwise, for Marilyn. Anthony Summers describes in his 1985 book *Goddess: The Secret Lives of Marilyn Monroe* how *New York Post* writer Sidney Skolsky, a legendary columnist standing a mere five feet (150cm) tall, strolled up to the water fountain and enjoyed a rather long wait behind a thirsty young woman with a shapely derriere. "He and the owner of the behind made jokes to each other about the capacity of camels, and ended up having a long conversation," Summers wrote. Thus Marilyn began an advantageous friendship that would last her lifetime; it was beneficial to Skolsky as well, for Marilyn frequently acted as his chauffeur (he had never bothered to learn how to drive).

While she cultivated friendships with Skolsky and other members of the press, demonstrating a keen intelligence about how to manipulate publicity, Marilyn's work prospects in 1947 didn't much improve. She did, however, finally make it onto a soundstage.

According to biographer Graham McCann, she received her first screen credit by virtue of her role as a switchboard operator in the Betty Grable musical *The Shocking Miss Pilgrim*. That year she also appeared as an extra in *Scudda Hoo! Scudda Hay!*, generally regarded as her first role, but much of that part wound up on the cutting-room floor before the film was shown in 1948. Her one line, "Hello," was reinstated in some versions after her death. Her role later that year in *Dangerous Years*, as a waitress in a café frequented by a teenage gang, gave her the chance to speak a couple of lines. Writer Sheilah Graham said this role was the result of Marilyn's badgering Ben Lyon, with whom she had a brief affair after he promised to help further her career. She reportedly also worked as an extra in a couple of other movies, which were forgettable—and forgotten.

As part of courting those in power who could someday help make her a star, Marilyn made it a point to attend as many Hollywood parties as she could, although she referred to this as "the hardest part of her campaign to make good." Before she could set aside enough from her low weekly salary to buy an evening gown—her stacks of bills for the extravagances she

One of Marilyn's early modeling shots, circa 1946.

bought on time payments kept her quite broke—she kept her distance from the glamorous stars. But when she finally could afford it, she bought a flaming red, low-cut gown, "and my arrival in it usually infuriated half the women present," she wrote. "I was sorry in a way to do this, but I had a long way to go, and I needed a lot of advertising to get there."

Her hope was to be noticed by the Hollywood reporters in attendance for mention in their columns or, perhaps even more importantly, by the studio executives who could influence her fortune. ("There was also the consideration that if my studio bosses saw me standing among the regular movie stars they might get to thinking of me as a star also.") One such boss whose attention she managed to capture in late 1947 was Joseph Schenck, a sixty-nine-year-old man of major influence at Twentieth Century-Fox. He was a founder of Twentieth-Century Pictures and had negotiated its merger with Fox in 1935. He also was a former husband of Norma Jeane's namesake, Norma Talmadge.

Quick with a smile for anyone who might be able to help her, Marilyn recognized Schenck in his limousine as he was leaving the studio and dazzled him enough that he had his driver stop, called Marilyn to the car, and handed her his telephone number. "Call me about dinner around this time next week," he said.

Marilyn became one of Schenck's stable of starlets whom he would invite to his mansion for social gatherings. "I went to Mr. Schenck's mansion the first few times because he was one of the heads of my studio," she wrote. "After that I went because I liked him…. I seldom spoke three words during dinner but would sit at Mr. Schenck's elbow and listen like a sponge." She also accepted those invitations because the meals at Schenck's mansion were bountiful and much needed.

The rumors that ensued about Marilyn being "Joe Schenck's girl" were the first bit of fame she enjoyed, and despite many stories insisting that their relationship was physical, Marilyn always denied that she and Schenck ever had sex. "Mr. Schenck never so much as laid a finger on my wrist, or tried to," she wrote. Marion Marshall, future wife of Robert Wagner and another of the starlets favored with invitations by Schenck, said of those visits to his mansion: "He was like a father figure to me, a father confessor, a very wise, lovely old man. When the evening was over, I would simply be taken home in the limousine, and so far as I know it was the same for Marilyn."

Joseph Schenck, shown here in 1941, took a special interest in Marilyn when they met in 1947.

However, Associated Press writer James Bacon, who met Marilyn in 1948 and claimed in a 1977 article to have slept with her at Schenck's guest cottage in 1949, said Marilyn did "look after" the elder man's sexual needs. He said they were interrupted in bed at the guest house one night by Schenck's butler, summoning Marilyn to the studio executive's bedroom, but that Marilyn soon returned, giggling that she had arrived at Schenck's bed too late.

Despite her friendship with a major influence at her studio, Marilyn's contract with Twentieth Century-Fox was terminated after just one year, in September 1947. She was told that she was being dismissed because Zanuck viewed her as unphotogenic. Her reaction was to go home and stay there, crying for days on end over being fired for the one thing she thought she had going for her: her looks. Her depression was exacerbated by the prospect that Schenck had played a part in the decision to terminate her contract. "I kept crying as if I were at a funeral burying Marilyn Monroe," she wrote of that bleak time.

Tommy Zahn, one of Marilyn's boyfriends during the summer of 1946 and a fellow stock player, told author Anthony Summers that Twentieth Century-Fox's rejection of Marilyn may have been linked to Zanuck's daughter. Zahn met Darrylin Zanuck while he worked as a beach lifeguard; the girl's crush on him led to an introduction to her father and a stock-player contract. He was fired at the same time as Marilyn and speculates that Zanuck disapproved of his involvement with her. Zahn said he believes he got his initial contract only because Zanuck had wanted to "groom him for marriage" to his daughter, then was quickly dropped when Zanuck saw that Zahn's interests did not include such a long-term relationship.

About a week after her contract termination, Marilyn's spirits were lifted by a telephone invitation to dinner at Schenck's mansion. There, she found her host surprised to learn she had lost her job the week before. He encouraged her to "keep going" and suggested she try her luck elsewhere.

To make ends meet and finance her recent enrollment at the Actors Lab in Hollywood, operated by Morris Carnovsky and his wife, Phoebe Brand, Marilyn returned to modeling. (At times, she would later admit to

Modeling helped Marilyn survive between studio contracts, since she refused to be "a kept woman."

allowance from his father. The two struck up a romance, but this ended when he allegedly found Marilyn in the bunk of his younger brother, Sydney, with whom he shared a bedroom. During this time, late autumn 1947, she had one of her many abortions (it is estimated that Marilyn had a dozen or more over the years), according to a close friend of Chaplin's. Yet she and Chaplin remained good friends until her death.

In the absence of acting work, Marilyn considered leaving Hollywood altogether for the first time in her life. As 1947 neared an end, Marilyn packed up a few belongings and was ready to hitchhike to San Francisco when actor John Carroll met her at a drive-in restaurant. She told him of her predicament, and he promised to help her if he could. So, hanging onto a new spark of hope, Marilyn remained in Los Angeles. She and Carroll met again before the end of the year, when Columbia had hired Marilyn as a "starlet caddy" for a celebrity golf tournament. This time Carroll was accompanied by his wife, Lucille Ryman, casting director for Metro-Goldwyn-Mayer.

The couple was won over by Marilyn's innocence, and her recounting of a recent near-assault made them determined to help her. Marilyn, who was now living in the home of a Burbank couple while they were away, claimed that a policeman, whom she had met earlier while she was out trying to cash a $40 check from her former studio job, had tried to break into her bedroom by cutting through a window screen. She ran from the house and called out for help, she said, and the police apprehended the intruder,

acting coach Lee Strasberg, her desperate financial situation also led her to work as a prostitute. Author Richard Lamparski claims in his book *Hidden Hollywood* that she also worked as a stripper for two weeks in 1948 at the Mayan Theatre in Los Angeles.)

Marilyn took to hanging out at Schwab's drugstore/coffee shop, a popular spot for out-of-work actors, although few of them could afford so much as a soda. One of these struggling actors was Charlie Chaplin, first son and namesake of the comic legend, who was squeaking by on a meager

During the first months of her Twentieth Century-Fox contract, Marilyn posed for endless publicity stills, among them this beach shot in February 1947 with her dog Ruffles.

who had returned to the scene. A search of the suspect revealed a police identification, and Marilyn said the officers there dissuaded her from filing charges because the young man had a wife and fourteen-month-old child. "So I didn't file any charges," she wrote. "Instead I moved out. I went back to a Hollywood bedroom, and I stayed in it for several days and nights without moving. I cried and stared out the window." The story was reported the next day in the *Hollywood Citizen-News*.

After hearing Marilyn's tale, Carroll told his wife that they had to "help this little girl." The couple began picking up many of Marilyn's expenses, and on December 4 they signed a personal-management contract with her. But her agent from Helen Ainsworth's firm, Harry Lipton, remained under contract and continued to collect his 10 percent share of her earnings. Marilyn soon moved into Carroll and Ryman's apartment, as the couple were often away overseeing the construction of a new home. But an alleged Peeping Tom incident at the apartment resulted in an invitation to live with the couple in their new home, also occupied by Carroll's mother.

Meanwhile, at the end of winter 1948, Joe Schenck called Columbia Pictures head Harry Cohn on Marilyn's behalf. The result was a six-month contract, to begin in March, with Columbia Pictures, a studio Marilyn had already been courting with little result. Columbia topped Marilyn's previous studio contract salary, offering her $125 a week. With a steady income again, Marilyn was able to move into a small Hollywood house. Friends advised her against taking the house because it supposedly was haunted, but the move was an escape from the tension between her and Carroll's mother, who disapproved of Marilyn's reluctance to wear clothing around the house (she probably also disapproved of Marilyn's desire to marry Carroll, a Clark Gable look-alike).

A full-figured Marilyn in 1947, about the time she was reported to have had an abortion following her affair with Charlie Chaplin, Jr., who became a lifelong friend.

Throughout her time at Columbia, Marilyn would move often, from the "haunted" house to a couple of Beverly Hills hotels and finally back to Studio Club. She continued to make lasting friends in the press, including James Bacon, who said of their first meeting in 1948: "We had lunch, and I tell you, she was the most exciting thing I'd ever talked to, and I've talked with all the big stars out there—you know, Joan Crawford, all of them. But something about Marilyn—she just had it. I went back to the AP office and I was going to write a story about her, a column. Well, my boss says, 'Who wants to read about a starlet?'"

Columbia provided Marilyn with a few more bit roles, including a chance to sing and dance while playing a poor girl ascending to stardom in *Ladies of the Chorus*. To help her play this part, the studio assigned its head drama coach, Natasha Lytess, and vocal coach Fred Karger—both of whom would also have a dramatic impact on Marilyn's personal life.

Lytess' first encounter with Marilyn left her far short of impressed. She viewed the starlet as "inhibited and cramped; she could not say a word freely." Marilyn's efforts to keep her upper lip lowered caused her to look unnatural when speaking, and her voice was "a piping sort of whimper," Lytess said later. But Marilyn was eager to learn and she came to rely heavily on Lytess for guidance and support, both in and out of class.

Marilyn already had opened a charge account at a nearby bookstore when she was awarded her Columbia contract, and Lytess intensified her zeal for reading to educate herself. Friends and acquaintances contend that Lytess was in love with Marilyn and that they had a lesbian affair. Even Marilyn confessed that she feared she might have lesbian tendencies because of her coldness toward having sex with men.

If Lytess was attracted to Marilyn sexually, this might be attributed in part to the young actress' nudist habits held over from her childhood. According to Lytess, Marilyn commonly would wander naked around the home they later shared—even when she was making breakfast in the kitchen. This immodesty also carried over to the studio, where she would readily shun clothes amid her crew of hairdressers, wardrobe staff, and makeup artists. "Being naked seems to soothe her—almost hypnotize her," Lytess said.

Billy Travilla, who was in charge of Marilyn's wardrobe for many of her films, confirmed Lytess' assessment. Travilla's first encounter with Marilyn in 1950 (he was twenty-four, she twenty-five) "was the sight of her

Marilyn with Natasha Lytess, who was assigned to be her acting coach for Ladies of the Chorus and remained in that role for seven years. To Lytess' expressed attraction for her pupil, Marilyn responded, "Don't love me, teach me."

in a black bathing suit," he said. "She opened the sliding doors of my fitting room, and a strap fell off, and her breast was exposed. She had a delightful quality, being so beautiful, of wanting to show herself. Some people were offended by it—and of course she did it on purpose. She was so childlike she could do anything, and you would forgive as you would forgive a 7 year old." Robert Slatzer also told of the delight Marilyn took in parading around completely naked in front of him, even when his friends were present.

Regarding Lytess' relationship with Marilyn, Lena Pepitone, Marilyn's New York maid from 1957 until her death, wrote in her memoirs, *Marilyn Monroe Confidential*, that her employer "had looked up to [Lytess], and when she made her advances, Marilyn simply accepted them as part of her training." But any doubts Marilyn might have had regarding her sexual preferences were swept away when she fell in love "for the first time" with Fred Karger.

Hours before the 1957 premiere of **The Prince and the Showgirl**, *which doubled as a benefit for the "Free Milk Fund for Babies," Marilyn took time for publicity shots to aid the cause with a toddler named William.*

In Marilyn's autobiography, she makes no mention of her vocal coach-student relationship with Karger at Columbia. Rather, she says, they were introduced after he caught her eye as she left an unsuccessful appointment with the casting department at MGM studios. Nonetheless, as her coach, Karger was attracted to Marilyn's vulnerability as well as her potential. When he found out how little food she had to sustain her—her usual diet consisted of raw hamburger meat and not much else—he invited her to his home for dinner.

The Karger home came to be a loving sanctuary for Marilyn. Karger introduced her to his mother, Anne, as "a little girl who's very lonely and broke." Anne embraced the starlet instantly, and the two formed a friendship that not only lasted the rest of Marilyn's life, but far outlasted Fred's

relationship with Marilyn. Fred's sister, Mary, proved to be an easy person for the starlet to talk with. (Karger's father, Max, had died twenty-seven years earlier, when his son was only five years old. He was one of the founders of MGM, and his wife had played hostess to the giant stars of the silent-picture era in Hollywood's early heyday.)

Mary's children, as well as Fred's from his failing marriage, adored Marilyn, whom they fondly recalled as "this vision…a beautiful blonde lady." During Marilyn's first marriage she spent a lot of time playing with children, mostly Dougherty's nephews, and her fondness for children and their games made her "part of our group of little friends," Mary's daughter, Anne, remembered. "She gave me a birthday party and sat there on the floor and played party games with us. We came to love her very much."

When Natasha Lytess had to move with her daughter from their Beverly Hills home due to reduced income, she took a Hollywood apartment that happened to be very near the Karger home. Marilyn moved out of her Studio Club room and into the apartment with Lytess to be closer to the family she had adopted.

Unfortunately, the man who had introduced Marilyn into his close-knit clan apparently did not love her. Although Karger's involvement with Marilyn began as his marriage was ending (Marilyn reportedly cried when he was divorced), Karger did not return her intensifying passion on an emotional level. Physically, he had no reserve about their relationship, and Marilyn later admitted that she had more than one abortion during their on-again, off-again affair.

"He grinned a lot when we were together and kidded me a lot," Marilyn wrote of Karger. "I knew he liked me and was happy to be with me. But his love didn't seem anything like mine. Most of his talk to me was a form of criticism. He criticized my mind. 'You cry too easily,' he'd say. 'That's because your mind isn't developed. Compared to your breasts, it's embryonic.' I couldn't contradict him because I had to look up that word in a dictionary."

When Karger finally relented to discuss what future they might have together, he told Marilyn that he couldn't marry her because of his son. He said that if anything happened to him, and his son had to be raised by Marilyn, "It wouldn't be right for him to be brought up by a woman like you." At that point, Marilyn forced herself to see that the affair had to end. "He didn't love me," she said. "A man can't love a woman for whom he feels half contempt. He can't love her if his mind is ashamed of her."

Repeatedly, Marilyn tried to leave Karger, but each time she said good-bye she would end up sobbing in his arms. "It's hard to do something that hurts your heart, especially when it's a new heart and you think that one hurt may kill it," she wrote. Karger, reflecting on their relationship

Marilyn got her first review when Ladies of the Chorus *came out in 1948. Critics panned the film, but praised Marilyn highly.*

years later, said, "I was torn myself and wondered, Could it work? Her ambition bothered me to a great extent. I wanted a woman who was a homebody. She might have thrown it all over for the right man." Yet this man wanting a homebody eventually married actress Jane Wyman, the former Mrs. Ronald Reagan—not once, but twice (the first time in 1952).

As Marilyn managed to stay away longer between each of her attempted breakups with Karger over the next couple of years, she finally mustered the strength to end the affair—although she did remain close to his mother, Anne. She did, however, retain Karger as her vocal coach. When *Ladies of the Chorus* came out in October 1948, the film itself got panned, but Marilyn got her first review—a positive endorsement in

Motion Picture Herald, by Tibor Krekes, who called her singing "one of the brightest spots" in the film. "She is pretty and, with her pleasing voice and style, she shows promise," he wrote of her delivery of the song "Every Baby Needs a Da Da Daddy." (Karger also may have helped Marilyn's career in part by finding a dentist who would help correct her slight overbite with a retainer at no cost.)

Before she had the pleasure of seeing this endorsement by Krekes, Marilyn would again endure having her contract terminated, this time after only six months at Columbia. According to Marilyn, this dismissal was the result of an encounter she had had with studio head Harry Cohn. She said the studio's casting director phoned to set up an afternoon appointment. Seeing this as her "big chance," for he "wouldn't have called me himself if it wasn't for a real part," Marilyn spent all day getting ready for the meeting. This preparation probably involved a long soak in the bathtub, repeated shampoos and stylings, and tedious makeup efforts, as such was her tendency for years to come. She would lose track of time while in the tub, savoring the perfumed waters because of the years during her childhood when she had to take baths in the same water as half a dozen others in her foster homes.

When Marilyn arrived, the casting director "wasn't in his office, but his secretary smiled at me to go inside and wait for him." While she waited for him, Cohn entered the room and invited her into his own office. There, she said, he showed her a picture of his yacht and informed her that she would be joining him for an overnight cruise; they would return just in time for him to make his wife's dinner party the next evening. Marilyn said she refused his invitation. Furious, Cohn yelled "This is your last chance!" as she left his office.

"I drove to my room in my car," Marilyn wrote of the aftermath. "Yes, there was something special about me, and I knew what it was. I was the

Marilyn's contract was terminated shortly before the opening of Ladies of the Chorus.

kind of girl they found dead in a hall bedroom with an empty bottle of sleeping pills in her hand." As for Cohn, his anger at being rejected by a young starlet he regarded as "Joe Schenck's girl" would pale in comparison with the anguish that would haunt him within a couple years after letting Marilyn Monroe escape from his studio.

So by September 1948, just a month before her favorable first review, Marilyn was again out of work. To make matters worse, her beloved Aunt Ana had died, reportedly of a heart attack after an extended illness. Once again Marilyn spent her days looking for modeling work, sometimes hanging out with the other unemployed actors at Schwab's.

September also brought her first professional encounter with photographer Tom Kelley, whose calendar shots of her the following year would eventually help boost her career.

While making the rounds of photographers' studios, Marilyn walked unannounced into the Tom Kelley Studio (she preferred face-to-face first encounters to the cold brush-offs models normally receive over the phone). It was a hot Saturday afternoon, and as she approached the desk of Kelley and his wife, Natalie, "her heart [sank]," wrote Marion Charles in the June 1991 *Los Angeles* magazine. Marilyn recognized Tom Kelley as the passerby who had loaned her $5 for cab fare two years earlier after she rear-ended the car of a priest as she hurried to the Bliss-Hayden Miniature Theatre (now The Beverly Hills Playhouse), where she had a role in a play. She hoped he didn't recognize her, because she had never repaid the loan.

Kelley and his wife exchanged glances that Marilyn read as the prelude to rejection, so in an urgent, intimate voice—that Kelley said he couldn't resist—she pleaded her case. Despite her somewhat gaudy appearance—Marilyn was wearing a tight skirt, a low-cut blouse, and high-heeled ankle-strap shoes, and her lipstick was very overdone—Kelley saw promise and asked her to change into a swimsuit, while Natalie accompanied her to the dressing room to tone down her look. The Marilyn who emerged from the dressing room won over the Kelleys, who gave her a modeling assignment for a beer billboard, which led to many more such jobs over the next several months. But when Tom asked Marilyn if she would be interested in posing for artistic nude shots for calendars, she turned him down. Unlike many starlets who posed for nude photographs and took roles in pornographic movies to survive before finding fame in Hollywood, Marilyn consistently refused such work, even if the money was good.

February 1949 brought Marilyn her reward for being able to exude sexuality without taking off her clothes. As her relationship with Karger was on its decline, producer Lester Cowan was looking for a sexy girl for a walk-on part in *Love Happy*, starring the Marx Brothers. Marilyn said she heard about the part while sitting in Schwab's, but Fred Guiles said her agent, Harry Lipton, had kindled Cowan's interest with film footage.

In any case, Marilyn went to the set and was introduced by Cowan to Groucho and Harpo Marx. Groucho asked her, "Can you walk?" She

The sexy walk associated with Marilyn made its debut in Love Happy, *a 1949 Marx Brothers film.*

After strutting her stuff during the audition for Love Happy, *Marilyn recalled that Groucho told her, "You have the prettiest ass in the business." Her reaction? "I'm sure he meant it in the nicest way."*

fully happy." Then her name appeared in Louella Parsons' movie column, which reported she was being put under contract by Cowan. Marilyn rushed to visit Cowan and told him she would like to sign the contract she had read about. There was no contract "yet," he told her, but the prospect inspired Marilyn to go to a jeweler and buy Karger a $500 watch, to be paid off over time, as the rest of her purchases always were. When Karger asked why she didn't have it engraved with her name or a sentiment, she replied, "Because you'll leave me someday." She wanted him to be able to use it even after he had found another lover.

Marilyn later heard from Cowan, but the rumor about a contract to sign was just that—a rumor. Instead, Cowan hired Marilyn to promote *Love Happy* on a nationwide tour beginning in summer 1950. Meanwhile, she returned to the photographers' studios so that she could pay the bills, including the $25 monthly debt recently incurred for the watch she had bought Karger.

Tom Kelley had been one of Marilyn's most consistent employers for the past few months, and when he called her in May 1949 with another job, she was glad to hear from him. After falling behind on her monthly payments on the used car on which she depended to job-hunt, the car was repossessed. "A movie job hunter without a car in Hollywood was like a fireman without a fire engine," Marilyn wrote. "There were at least a dozen studios and agents' offices you had to visit every day. And they were in a dozen different districts, miles away from each other."

So when Kelley called Marilyn into his studio and told her that the modeling job was a nude calendar shot, she did not refuse as she always had. She told Kelley and his wife about the repossession of her car, and that the $50 they were offering her was the exact amount she needed to get it back. Kelley assured Marilyn that the shot would be done like a work of art, that he doubted she would be recognized as the model, and that no pelvic shots could be used. After weighing the pros and cons, Marilyn called the next morning and agreed to pose nude. Kelley, sensing that she was still hesitant, scheduled the shoot for 9 P.M. the same day.

nodded. He gave her the gist of the part: "This role calls for a young lady who can walk by me in such a manner as to arouse my elderly libido and cause smoke to issue from my ears." She walked. Groucho told her the result was "Mae West, Theda Bara and Bo Peep all rolled into one." Harpo honked his horn, whistled, and told Marilyn not to "do any walking in any unpoliced areas." She reported to the set for filming the next morning, to deliver her walk and a couple of Garbo-flavored lines—"I want you to help me" and "Some men are following me"—all of which amounted to only about ninety seconds of film footage.

For the next week, as she "sat every evening listening to my lover argue about my various shortcomings," Marilyn said she "remained bliss-

Arriving on time that evening, Marilyn was asked to change into a robe in the dressing room so that the waistband marks from her jeans would fade before shooting began. Kelley set up the shot, securing his ladder and camera for the ceiling-to-floor angle of the red drape spread out below. After completing all the shot preparations, Kelley put on a recording, Cole Porter's "Begin the Beguine," and Marilyn, wearing nothing but her red high heels, entered the studio, giggling. With only Kelley, his wife, and his brother Bill in the room, the session was under way. After positioning Marilyn so that none of her pubic hair was showing, Kelley finally stopped giving her directions altogether, amazed at her ability to sense what poses were most appropriate.

Marilyn wrote of that session: "I was a little confused at first, and something kept nudging me in my [brain]. Sitting naked in front of a camera and striking joyous poses reminded me of the dreams I used to have as a child. I felt sad that this should be the only dream I ever had to come true. After a few poses the depression left me." But thoughts kept "nudging" her about how the photographs might affect her future as an actress.

After the shoot, the Kelleys took Marilyn, who hadn't eaten much over the past few days, out for a late chili meal. Kelley finally found out the real reason Marilyn agreed to do the nude shots: it was her way of showing her gratitude. She reminded Kelley of the car accident and revealed that she was the girl to whom he had loaned $5 for cab fare. She then signed the model release under an assumed name: Mona Monroe.

"I had my car back the next day and was able to romp around from studio to studio and enjoy the usual quota of snubs," Marilyn said. As for Kelley, he sold two prints for a total of $900 to Western Lithograph Company, and these were published in its "Miss Golden Dreams" calendar. After nearly being banned from the mail—the post office considered it pornographic, and its sale was outlawed in at least two states—the calendar soon turned

Western Lithograph a profit of close to $1,000,000—even before the model was identified. No one knew that Marilyn Monroe was "Miss Golden Dreams" until she was on the verge of stardom nearly three years later; the calendar has made millions since that time.

MARILYN

PHOTOGRAPH BY TOM KELLEY
FROM THE FAMED RED VELVET CALENDAR SESSION

The still-struggling Marilyn finally got the call from Cowan to embark on a publicity tour for *Love Happy*. With all travel expenses paid and a salary of $100 per week, Marilyn left behind her deteriorating relationship with Karger in June 1949 and set out for New York, the first stop on the tour. With a $75 wardrobe allowance from Cowan, Marilyn bought three wool suits for the trip; she knew that New York and some of the other stops were in the North and she pictured a snow-blanketed clime. "In my excitement over going to see these great cities for the first time I forgot it was summertime there as well as in Los Angeles," Marilyn wrote. "When the train stopped in New York I could hardly breathe, it was so hot." She said her wool suit made her "feel as if [she were] wearing an oven."

Turning the starlet's hot predicament into a publicity asset, Cowan's press agent had her photographed on the train steps, "perspiration running down my face and an ice cream cone in each hand." The photograph was released with the caption: "Marilyn Monroe, the hottest thing in pictures, cooling off." The "cooling off" theme continued back at the hotel, where she changed into a bathing suit for more photographs—a cycle that would repeat itself for the remainder of her trip.

While in New York, Marilyn was interviewed by show-business columnist Earl Wilson, who introduced her to the East Coast as the "Mmmmmm Girl." She also was reunited with Andre de Dienes, who took her to the beach for a photo session. And a chance meeting at El Morocco, an exclusive Manhattan nightclub, brought her a friend for life in Henry Rosenfeld, a thirty-eight-year-old millionaire and dress manufacturer. When Marilyn entered El Morocco, she apparently caught Rosenfeld's eye and was invited to join him on the "right" side of the club. They supposedly became lovers years

The summer promotion tour for **Love Happy** *featured* **Marilyn trying to keep her cool at every stop.**

later, and Rosenfeld confided: "Marilyn thought sex got you closer, made you a closer friend. She told me she hardly ever had an orgasm, but she was very unselfish. She tried above all to please the opposite sex. Ah, but it wasn't just sex. She could be so happy and gay. How I remember that laughter!" Rosenfeld would later help her find doctors, offer a sympathetic ear, and attempt to sort out her finances.

Marilyn continued her "exploitation" tour in Detroit, Cleveland, Chicago, Milwaukee, and Rockford, Illinois, but her enjoyment was tempered by the fact that she was penniless: Cowan's bookkeeping department was unable to keep up with the tour, so she had received none of her salary and had no money for personal spending. In Rockford, she told the tour press agent that she was very eager to return to Hollywood. "The tour, in a way, was a failure," Marilyn wrote. "When I got back I didn't seem to have any more to talk about than before. And absence didn't seem to have made [Karger's] heart grow any fonder."

Upon her return in August, Marilyn got a small part, with the help of Ben Lyon, in a Twentieth Century-Fox western, *A Ticket to Tomahawk*. The movie came out in May 1950, a few months after *Love Happy*, but Marilyn's role was lost amid a chorus of girls being shuffled through violent Colorado Indian country. But the sexy walk she unveiled in the midst of Marx Brothers mayhem in *Love Happy* brought her great attention from the press. Her promotional tour had given her much-needed public exposure and also helped capture the interest of the powerful William Morris Agency.

Harry Lipton got a call from Morris agent Johnny Hyde, who asked for details on his contract with Marilyn. Lipton saw Hyde's interest as Marilyn's big chance, and he did nothing to stand in the way. He accepted Hyde's offer to take over as Marilyn's agent. The terms of their agreement and Lipton's compensation are not clear.

Hyde first met Marilyn in Palm Springs at the Racquet Club when she returned from her 1949 summer tour. Hyde had just seen *Love Happy* at a private screening. They talked for a while, and he gave her his card. Once he made his arrangements with Lipton, he set out with all of his energy to make Marilyn a star. (When Hyde met Marilyn, he was fifty-three, thirty years her senior. He was also wealthy, married, and suffering from a heart condition that would take his life less than two years later. Many would blame his death on his all-consuming efforts to further Marilyn's career.)

Modeling jobs were Marilyn's primary source of income until autumn 1949.

"You're going to be a great star," Hyde told Marilyn during their first formal meeting soon afterward at his Beverly Hills office. And Hyde would have known: among his "discoveries" were Lana Turner, Betty Hutton, and Rita Hayworth, and he helped make singer Al Jolson a millionaire. Comparing her with his other clients, he told Marilyn: "You're better. You'll go further. You've got more." Marilyn asked him why, if she was so much better, she couldn't make enough money to buy food. "It's hard for a star to get an eating job," Hyde replied. "A star is only good as a star. You don't fit into anything less." One can only wonder at how right his assessment of her was.

The first benefit of Marilyn's relationship with Hyde was the end of her continual rounds to find employment. Hyde undertook that laborious task, which left Marilyn free to concentrate on acting classes and reading. There were other benefits, too. Even at their first meeting, Hyde took her for lunch at the prestigious Romanoff's, and then to Saks Fifth Avenue in Beverly Hills to expand her wardrobe. Hyde's secretary said that he eventually spent thousands of dollars escorting Marilyn around Hollywood to make her better known. While Hyde also devoted much time to his handful of other clients during the day, all of his spare time was spent promoting Marilyn. His efforts cost him much more than time and money—eventu-

ally his marriage of twenty years to Mozelle Hyde, an exotic beauty in her own right who bore him four sons, was destroyed.

As Hyde fell in love with Marilyn, who was barely older than his eldest son, his wife confronted him about his feelings. He answered her honestly: "It's happened, and I can't do anything about it." But Marilyn, even though trying to end her unfulfilling relationship with Karger, had no such feelings for Hyde. She even rejected his repeated marriage proposals, saying that such a union wouldn't be fair to him. He countered that it wouldn't be a long marriage because of his heart condition, and that as his widow, she stood to inherit millions. But Marilyn said she could marry only for love, and that she did not love him. "I'll not leave you. I'll never betray you. But I can't marry you," she said.

Marilyn obviously had a strong affection for Hyde, and she said of their relationship: "Kindness is the strangest thing to find in a lover—or in anybody. No man had ever looked on me with such kindness. He not only knew me, he knew Norma Jeane too. He knew all the pain and all the desperate things in me. When he put his arms around me and said he loved me, I knew it was true. Nobody had ever loved me like that. I wished with all my heart that I could love him back…. But I felt everything else toward Johnny Hyde, and I was always happy to be with him."

Despite repeated letdowns, Hyde devoted himself fully to Marilyn. But also at work for the budding actress was her old friend Lucille Ryman, casting director for MGM who not only had helped Marilyn two years before, but had forgiven her advances toward her husband, John Carroll. Ryman came across a film role at MGM that seemed to have been written for Marilyn. She called up Hyde, sent him a copy of the script, and helped arrange for Marilyn's screen test. The role was that of a young mistress to a failing lawyer twice her age. The movie, *The Asphalt Jungle*, would be a springboard for Marilyn's career.

Marilyn convinced Natasha Lytess to coach her, and the two sequestered themselves for an entire weekend to work. Early the next week, accompanied by Hyde and Lytess, Marilyn met with the film's director,

John Huston. Huston was already familiar with the actress from her days at Columbia. He had intended to arrange a screen test with her even then, but cost considerations stopped his plans. Marilyn, for her part, was so nervous about facing the renowned Huston, whose films of note included *The Maltese Falcon,* that she was almost too terrified to respond to his questions, much less speak her lines.

"I felt sick," Marilyn recalled. "I had told myself a million times that I was an actress. I had practiced acting for years. Here, finally, was my first chance at a real acting part with a great director to direct me. And all I could do is stand with quivering knees and a quivering stomach and nod my head like a wooden toy."

When pressed to proceed with her lines, Marilyn asked if she could read the part lying on the floor. She had rehearsed reclined on a couch, as the script called for, so the floor "was almost the same thing." When she finished her lines, "Marilyn looked very insecure about the whole thing and asked to do it over," Huston recalled. "I agreed. But I had already decided on the first take. The part of Angela was hers."

With Marilyn hired for her first role in a major, A-grade movie, Lytess quit her job at Columbia to devote more time to coaching the nervous actress. To supplement her income, Lytess offered private lessons to other actors when she wasn't on the set with her dependent charge. Lytess' presence on the set of *The Asphalt Jungle* and Huston's encouraging direction saw Marilyn through her extreme nervousness during filming. Huston managed to elicit just the performance he had hoped for; when the film came out in June 1950, critics applauded the work's realism and often singled out Marilyn for her contributions. Yet when the film had its premiere at Grauman's Egyptian Theater, Marilyn did not attend. But among those on hand to observe the stars' arrival was her former husband, Jim Dougherty, now a Los Angeles policeman who had been assigned to restrain the crowd.

Although Marilyn's performance delighted MGM executives, Hyde was unable to secure a contract from the studio for her, so he took his favorite client back to Twentieth Century-Fox, where Joseph Mankiewicz was casting for a new Bette Davis film, *All About Eve.* The part—again a mistress—was small, but was a crucial stepping-stone for Marilyn's career,

---

Hometown Story, an hour-long industrial film, was one of Marilyn's half dozen bit roles in 1950.

for it helped her procure a new contract with the studio that first signed her and gave her a new name. Hyde negotiated the contract, which ensured a beginning salary of $500 a week, and was to cap at $1,500 per week over a seven-year period. Nevertheless, Marilyn was soon discontent, for she was beginning to resent being typecast in dumb-blonde roles. She was forced to take bit roles again in films including *The Fireball*, a Mickey Rooney "rollerdome" flick in which she had no lines; *Right Cross*, starring Dick Powell and June Allyson; and *Hometown Story*, a newspaper drama written and directed by Arthur Pierson, with whom she had made *Dangerous Years*. Her acting kept her busy in 1950, but she was quite far from satisfied.

During the filming of *All About Eve*, the "Red Scare" influence on Hollywood made itself painfully apparent to Marilyn. Her habit of bringing books to the studio had already been established, but the one she read on the set of *All About Eve* brought stern warnings from Mankiewicz. When he saw that she was poring over the autobiography of Lincoln Steffens, the American muckraking journalist whose critical writings reflected the plight of the poor, he warned her that she was certain to get into trouble by being viewed as a political radical. "I couldn't imagine anybody picking on me because I admired Lincoln Steffens," Marilyn wrote of that encounter. "The only other political figure I'd ever admired was Abraham Lincoln. I used to read everything I could find about him." (Marilyn's admiration for Lincoln was evident from the picture of him that she always hung on the wall of her home, and the copy of the Gettysburg Address that she kept near it. Author Anthony Summers called this intense reverence "her first love affair with a president of the United States.")

Thinking that Mankiewicz was off-base with his advice, Marilyn again made her admiration for Steffens known, this time to the studio's publicity department. She had been asked to list the ten greatest men in the world; Steffens topped her list. The publicity department told her that they'd have to omit Lincoln Steffens, as they didn't want anyone investigating her. The point hit home, and Marilyn stopped mentioning the radical Steffens in conversation. Instead, she continued to secretly read his autobiography, including the second volume, and kept both books hidden under her bed.

By the time *All About Eve* was released in November 1950, Marilyn's desire to assume more serious roles was being mocked in the press. The fact that she got any press at all, however, indicated that her popularity was rising. Hyde had helped turn her fortunes around, but the Marilyn Monroe image the public embraced—that of a blonde bombshell with comedic talents, not an actress to be taken too seriously—would be one she could not shake as it took on a life of its own.

Late 1950 brought Marilyn more critical attention, and it also brought a deterioration in Hyde's health. Hyde's influence over Marilyn had extended to her physical attributes: he persuaded her to undergo minor plastic surgery to add cartilage to her jaw to make her chin line stronger (some who knew her also claim her nose was altered). In addition, he talked her into moving out of her Beverly Carlton studio apartment and into his home, which was near that of his former wife and their children. This move infuriated Hyde's family, and the arrangement did not last very long.

"One evening in his home he started up the stairs to get me a book," Marilyn wrote. "I saw him stop on the landing and lean against the balustrade…. A week later Johnny Hyde began asking me again to marry him. He had been to a doctor, and the doctor had told him he didn't have long to live." Hyde was admitted to Cedars of Lebanon Hospital (now Cedars-Sinai Medical Center) in early December, as he had suffered a mild coronary occlusion. His hospital stay lasted no more than four days, and he planned a trip to Palm Springs upon his release. Before leaving, according to author Fred Guiles, Hyde arranged with his business manager Sam Berke to have his will changed to provide for Marilyn, even though she still refused to marry him. He then left for the Racquet Club in Palm Springs, confident that the changes to his will would be made.

Hyde, seemingly aware of his impending death and too anxious to be left alone, took his secretary, Dona Holloway, to Palm Springs with him. After four days there, and no improvement in Hyde's health, Holloway—eager to return to her husband at home—summoned Marilyn, who had just recovered from her plastic surgery and was preparing for the role of a secretary in her next film, *As Young As You Feel*. Marilyn pledged to leave for

Marilyn met Arthur Miller and immediately became enamored with him during the filming of As Young As You Feel *in late 1950. This photograph is from one of her scenes in the film.*

Arthur Miller (left) with his close friend Elia Kazan, with whom Marilyn was rumored to have had an affair in 1950 or 1951.

Palm Springs as soon as she had fulfilled her commitments. On December 16, she drove directly from the studio to the Racquet Club for what was to become a deathwatch. There, she witnessed Hyde's final heart attack on December 17. She followed the ambulance back to Cedars of Lebanon Hospital in Los Angeles, and was at his side when he died the next day.

After his death, Hyde's family evicted Marilyn from his home and tried to bar her from the funeral, but she wouldn't stay away. At one point she threw herself onto his casket, sobbing inconsolably and calling his name. "I wished I was dead with him," she later wrote. "I was without his importance to fight for me and without his love to guide me." From Hyde's home, she went into seclusion at Natasha Lytess' apartment.

The day after the funeral, Lytess said she returned home to find Marilyn unconscious—her cheeks "puffed out like an adder's" from a mouthful of sleeping pills she had not yet swallowed. Marilyn had left one note on Lytess' pillow, which read: "I leave my car and fur stole to Natasha." She left another note outside her bedroom door that asked that Lytess' daughter not be allowed to enter. Through Lytess' intervention, Marilyn had failed at her third suicide attempt. (Marilyn later confessed to

writer Ben Hecht of two other suicide attempts as a teenager—one time she tried to gas herself, the other time she took sleeping pills.) A few years later, Marilyn spoke about her lingering feelings of guilt and sorrow regarding Johnny Hyde with her New York maid, Lena Pepitone: "If I had married him, maybe he could have lived. He used to say I was the only one who could save his life."

Twentieth Century-Fox, sympathizing with their grief-stricken costar, tolerated a few days of seclusion. But when Marilyn returned to the set of *As Young As You Feel*, she was still very much in mourning. There, in a studio warehouse to which she would often retreat to cry, Marilyn's grief was observed by playwright Arthur Miller, who within six years would become her husband. Miller was visiting the film's director, Harmon Jones, with Elia Kazan, who had met Marilyn a few months before Hyde's death. (The following year, Kazan would earn much acclaim for his film *A Streetcar Named Desire*.)

Marilyn's sorrow touched Miller, a thirty-five-year-old father of two who had married his college sweetheart, Mary Slattery. The playwright had won a Pulitzer Prize the year before for *Death of a Salesman*, and Marilyn

Left: Marilyn in a publicity still for the 1951 film Love Nest. *Opposite: The poster for* Love Nest *gave Marilyn her first prominent billing, which she earned with a standout performance.*

already was an admirer. Even after their brief first meeting, and another just days later at a party given by Charles Feldman, who later would become Marilyn's new agent, Lytess said that she "could tell Marilyn was in love with him…. It showed in the way she acted."

At Feldman's party, Miller and Marilyn conversed privately. Marilyn told Lytess, "It was like running into a tree! You know—like a cool drink when you've got a fever." Miller was equally impressed; he sent Marilyn a long letter later that week. Marilyn had revealed at the party that she was looking for someone to admire, and Miller proposed in the letter that she admire Abraham Lincoln, recommending that she read Carl Sandburg's biography on the president. Of course, Marilyn had been an admirer of Lincoln since she was a schoolgirl, and years later, her interest would lead her to meet and befriend Sandburg. (Sandburg lamented upon their meeting: "Too bad I'm forty-eight years too old.")

Miller and Marilyn corresponded by letter during 1951, and over the next three years Marilyn would meet with Miller about a half dozen times when she was on the East Coast. The two eventually lost touch, with Miller trying to keep his rocky marriage alive (Mary Miller would later contend that their eventual divorce had nothing to do with Miller's relationship with Marilyn) and Marilyn becoming engrossed in her work and new relationships.

Despite her grief over Hyde, Marilyn won critical praise for her work in *As Young As You Feel*. The role was not that big, but Marilyn had benefited from good lines and the capable direction of Harmon Jones. Afterward, she immediately went to work on her next film, *Love Nest*, in early 1951. Marilyn rose above the bland work of most of her costars (which included former *Tonight* host Jack Paar, who criticized Marilyn's habit of carrying around "pretentious" literature), prompting Fred Guiles to praise her: "Whatever flavor the film possessed was given it by Frank Fay, who played a rascal with decent instincts, and Marilyn, who emerged from this production as an actress able to instill more excitement into a role than it deserved."

Marilyn's performance was not the only noteworthy aspect of her employment at Twentieth Century-Fox following Hyde's death. According to her agents, just as much effort was expended to get her to the studio each morning, for she was becoming increasingly dependent on pills to help her sleep. (In fact, Marilyn became increasingly notorious for her lateness as her career progressed, particularly

as her drug and alcohol use rose to alarmingly high levels.) After meeting indifference from the offices of William Morris after Hyde's death, Marilyn turned to Famous Artists for representation. The agency was headed by Charles Feldman, who had acquired a reputation on par with that of Hyde, and Marilyn was impressed with Famous Artists agent Hugh French.

When not at work on a film, Marilyn worked doggedly to improve her acting skills. Lytess devoted major energies toward this end, because Marilyn had made sure that her trusted coach had followed her to Twentieth Century-Fox. But Marilyn also sought the help of Michael Chekhov, son of Russian playwright Anton Chekhov and former student of famed Moscow Art Theatre instructor Konstantin Stanislavsky. Chekhov preferred to teach only the classics, and Marilyn saw working with him as a chance to finally be perceived as a serious actress. Her studies with Chekhov excluded Lytess, on whom she now relied mostly for script assistance and whose presence she constantly required—mostly to bolster her confidence—on the set. Marilyn became a Chekhov student in the fall of 1951, and within months she was playing Cordelia to his King Lear. She impressed her teacher with her portrayal, and he reinforced her belief that her film roles were well beneath her acting capabilities.

Marilyn told an interviewer about an incident with her teacher during a scene from *The Cherry Orchard*: Chekhov stopped the action to ask Marilyn if she had been preoccupied with sex during her performance. She answered no, to which he countered, "All through our playing of that scene I kept receiving sex vibrations from you…. You are a young woman who gives off sex vibrations—no matter what you are doing or thinking. And your studio bosses are only interested in your sex vibrations. I see now why they refuse to regard you as an actress. You are more valuable to them as a sex stimulant." To this Marilyn succinctly retorted, "I want to be an artist, not an

Regarding her choice of sleepwear:

Q.:

What do you wear to bed, Marilyn?

M.:

Chanel No. 5.

erotic freak. I don't want to be sold to the public as a celluloid aphrodisiac. It was all right for the first few years. But now it's different."

While working to expand her acting skills in 1951, Marilyn also enrolled in adult extension classes, studying literature and art appreciation with a focus on the Renaissance. "I went to school every afternoon and often in the evening," Marilyn wrote of the experience. "The teacher was a woman. I was depressed by this at first because I didn't think a woman could teach me anything. But in a few days I knew differently."

This attitude that women had little to contribute may have been a consequence of her upbringing, author Gloria Steinem observed in *Marilyn*, as the starlet had mostly tragic figures for female role models. Only Ana Lower met Marilyn's standard for unconditional love. Also, while Marilyn was grateful to Grace Goddard after she realized the sacrifices she had made in becoming her legal guardian, Marilyn felt betrayed by Grace for sending her to the orphanage and arranging her marriage to Dougherty. Marilyn also later told some of her friends that she had given birth to a son as the result of rape by a foster father, and that Grace had forced her to give it up for adoption. This contention has never been substantiated.

Marilyn's contacts with women in Hollywood were no better. Marilyn was a fairly silent partner in numerous feuds with actresses. The more notable detractors were Zsa Zsa Gabor, who claimed Marilyn was making advances toward her husband, George Sanders, and Joan Crawford, who denounced Marilyn's "vulgar" appearance.

Marilyn had first met Crawford at a dinner at Joe Schenck's house. Crawford, dressed in an elegant gown, was critical of Marilyn's choice of a white knit dress for dinner attire. "Taste is every bit as important as looks and figure," she told the young starlet before offering to help her improve her wardrobe. They decided to meet on a Sunday. "It turned out that Miss Crawford and I went to the same church," Marilyn said, and after services, Marilyn followed Crawford to her home, hoping to be given some of the mighty actress' discarded gowns. Instead, Crawford told Marilyn that if she would make a list of all her clothes, she would tell her "all the things you need to buy and see that you buy the right things."

"For some reason I couldn't tell Miss Crawford that she had seen my wardrobe in full—the incorrect white knitted dress and the wrong gray suit [that she had worn to church]," Marilyn said. Marilyn was simply too embarrassed to compile the wardrobe list, and besides a brief phone call to the agitated Crawford to tell her that she hadn't done so, she wrote that "the next time I heard from Miss Crawford was in the newspapers. This was a year later. I'd gone to work at Twentieth Century-Fox again, and the Marilyn Monroe boom had started.... Among the honors that were now showering on me was the privilege of presenting one of the Oscars to one of the award winners at the Academy's annual affair" in March 1951. The recipient was Thomas Moulton; the award was Best Sound Recording for *All About Eve*.

"When my turn came I managed to reach the platform, say my piece, and return to my table without any mishap," Marilyn said. "Or so I thought, until I read Joan Crawford's remarks in the morning papers. She said that Marilyn Monroe's vulgar performance at the Academy affair was a disgrace to all of Hollywood. The vulgarity, she said, consisted of my wearing a dress too tight for me and wriggling my rear when I walked up holding one of the holy Oscars in my hand."

Such publicity aside, demands on her time, including a new film role, forced Marilyn to abandon her academic studies. She vowed, however, "that in a few years after things had settled down I would start learning—everything. I would read all the books and find out about all the wonders there were in the world. And when I sat among people I would not only understand what they were talking about, I'd be able to contribute a few words."

When she finally got a taste of success, Marilyn (seen here in a 1952 photograph) became a target for such Hollywood notables as Joan Crawford and Zsa Zsa Gabor.

Marilyn would abandon her ambitions to further her classroom education, but she rarely let slide her attentions to the powerful press. She won over *Look*'s West Coast editor, Rupert Allan (he soon became her press agent) when they met in 1951; by October she had graced the magazine's cover. Allan's counterpart at *Collier's* was Ted Strauss, and his first meeting with Marilyn left him in equal awe. Twentieth Century-Fox warned Strauss that Marilyn was terrified at the prospect of doing interviews and suggested he take her out to dinner to put her at ease. "I came away from that dinner so impressed," he recalled. "She was terribly bright and perceptive. She was doing what she thought people wanted her to do, but unsure—desperately trying to deal with where she came from." In addition, *Collier's* in September 1951 became the first national magazine to run a feature article on Marilyn, calling her "Hollywood's 1951 Model Blonde."

While she wooed the press and worked on her craft, Marilyn began to exert some of the independence she had cast off during her time with Hyde. She moved out of Lytess' home and found a tiny apartment. She usually lived alone there, but for a few months she shared her residence with another young actress, Shelley Winters, whom she had met years earlier at a charity baseball game and had seen often at Schwab's drugstore in her earliest starlet days. Winters described what it was like living with the woman-child Marilyn: "When you went to the john, she'd think you'd disappeared and she'd been left alone. She'd open up the door to see if you were still there. She was a little child."

The "child" and her friend were compatible roommates—both were unfulfilled at love and angry at the studio system. Winters said that Marilyn initiated an interesting exercise when she observed how nice it would be if women, like men, were able to count trips to the bedroom with attractive men as triumphs and not be expected to get emotionally involved. Both women proceeded to list all the famous men they would like to bed, and Winters said that Marilyn's list included Arthur

Miller, Albert Einstein, Elia Kazan, Jean Renoir, Lee Strasberg, John Huston, Ernest Hemingway, and Yves Montand, among others. In all, Marilyn listed seventeen men; more than half of those she later came to know personally, and a smaller fraction became her lovers.

As for her career, 1951 had been very kind to Marilyn. Her personal insecurities after Hyde's death did not hinder her progress regarding public popularity. Her workload was steady but left enough time for her acting studies, and her salary had been raised to $750 a week. She was the queen of pinups for U.S. soldiers worldwide, known as "Miss Cheesecake of 1951." But such successes did not satisfy Marilyn. Part of her dissatisfaction could be traced to her longing for paternal contact, because in autumn she phoned Lytess and asked her to accompany her to Hemet, a rural area near Palm Springs. She said she had tracked down her father and intended to go see him.

C. Stanley Gifford had established a dairy on ten acres (4ha) in Hemet; a private detective hired by Marilyn had located him. With Lytess at her side, Marilyn intended to drive there and arrive unannounced, but suddenly she changed her mind about halfway to Hemet and decided to phone ahead to say she was coming to visit. According to Marilyn, Gifford's phone was answered by a woman, who passed on his message that he didn't want to see her and that if she had "some complaint" with him she could contact his lawyer in Los Angeles. Marilyn got back in her car and drove home without saying a word. This scenario also was played out in front of Marilyn's good friend Sidney Skolsky, except that Skolsky said she went to the door of a house before being turned away.

Professionally, however, Marilyn's life was far more successful. In autumn, her third 1951 film, *Let's Make It Legal*, was being edited, and she was preparing for the comedy *We're Not Married*, which would be a huge box office hit in 1952. She also was on loan to another major studio, RKO, for *Clash by Night*, her most sophisticated film up until *Let's Make It Legal*. Unlike the gold digger she portrayed in *Let's Make It Legal*, Marilyn's naive fish-cannery worker in *Clash by Night*

Marilyn as a naive fish-cannery worker in **Clash by Night,** *1951.*

In 1951 Marilyn made one sophisticated film after another. First, she made Clash by Night *(opposite), then* Let's Make It Legal *(above), and finally, the box office smash* We're Not Married *(right).*

When it was revealed in March 1952 that Marilyn was the "Miss Golden Dreams" calendar girl, she made the cover of seventeen magazines.

had critics raving when the film opened in February 1952; the positive publicity the film generated also came at a most opportune time.

The year 1951 ended uneventfully for Marilyn, who apparently spent New Year's Eve alone in her apartment. Happily, 1952 was another good year, one that brought glowing successes, although it began beneath a cloud of scandal.

The official account of the potentially disastrous "Miss Golden Dreams" exposé was that Universal Press International reporter Aline Mosby discovered that the face and body on the 1950 calendar was that of rising star Marilyn Monroe. The press jumped all over the story, and Twentieth Century-Fox was hounded by journalists who wanted confirmation. Marilyn reportedly wanted to admit all, and the studios of her current pictures were on the verge of abandoning her. But Marilyn turned the scandal into a publicity coup by spinning a tale of woe—she lamented about being in dire financial need, saying she didn't have enough money to pay her rent—and responded with humor to the reporters' endless inquiries.

But the true account, according to biographer Anthony Summers, is that Marilyn broke the story as a publicity ploy. He reports in his book *Goddess* that Marilyn, with the help of her journalist friend Sidney Skolsky, arranged to be interviewed by Mosby. Johnny Campbell, one of the studio's publicity agents who sat in on the interview, said that Marilyn "asked Aline to follow her into the ladies' room, making as though she was having some sort of menstrual mishap." Once inside, Marilyn "proceeded to identify herself as the heroine of the calendar picture," Campbell said.

When Mosby's story broke in March 1952 identifying Marilyn as "Miss Golden Dreams," Marilyn acted surprised. Afterward, her witty retorts to reporters' questions ("Didn't you have anything on?" "Just the radio.") and her justifications ("Sure I posed. I was hungry.") actually improved her public image. The calendar also popped up time and again to intensify the publicity windfall it inspired.

Marilyn wrote of this time: "There are many other ways for a young and pretty girl to make $50 in Hollywood without any danger of being 'exposed.' I guess the public knew this. Somehow the story of the nude calendar pose didn't reflect scandal on me. It was accepted by the public for what it was, a ghost out of poverty rather than sin risen to haunt me."

March had come in like a lion for Marilyn, but it didn't go out like a lamb; she was too often in the spotlight to enjoy much serenity as winter passed into spring. She was featured on the April 7 cover of *Life* magazine, which declared her "the genuine article." She was preparing for work on a new comedy film, *Monkey Business*, starring Cary Grant, Ginger Rogers, and Charles Coburn, and had a bit part as a prostitute in *O. Henry's Full House*, a film montage of five short stories. Also, an encounter that spring eventually put her life into a frenzy of emotions and public notoriety: she met a thirty-seven-year-old boy of summer whose popularity would make her newfound fame pale in comparison.

Joe DiMaggio stepped into Marilyn's life in April 1952, marking the beginning of a tumultuous yet enduring relationship.

Joe DiMaggio didn't much care for what the press had to say, unless it had to do with sports. He had just retired from baseball the year before, after attaining the status of legend and billing as one of the greatest athletes the world had known. But a newspaper photograph that caught his eye changed his world. There, posed at a training session with Chicago White Sox players Joe Dobson and Gus Zernial, was a twenty-five-year-old beauty in short shorts named Marilyn Monroe. DiMaggio was not familiar with the rising star, but he had an affinity for actresses. His former wife, Dorothy Arnold, was an actress, and although that marriage didn't endure, she bore him a son, Joe Jr., whom he adored.

DiMaggio knew business agent David March, who was hoping to gain a client in the up-and-coming Marilyn, and he asked March to arrange a blind date. After much resistance, being more attracted to intellectuals than to jocks, Marilyn finally agreed to meet March, his date Peggy Rabe (a friend of Marilyn's), and DiMaggio for dinner.

"It was a balmy night, and I was late as usual," Marilyn wrote of their first meeting in April 1952. Actually, she was more than two hours late, first claiming to have forgotten about the meeting (Fred Guiles writes that she already had changed into her blue jeans and was "relaxing over a martini"), then saying she was too tired and unpresentable to join them. After much coaxing from Peggy, she finally arrived at the restaurant and was pleasantly surprised at what awaited her.

"I had thought I was going to meet a loud, sporty fellow," Marilyn wrote. "Instead I found myself smiling at a reserved gentleman in a gray suit, with a gray tie and a sprinkle of gray in his hair. There were a few blue polka dots in his tie. [Marilyn remembered the tie incorrectly; it was a blue-and-white latticework design. See the photograph on page 91.] If I hadn't been told he was some sort of a ballplayer, I would have guessed he was either a steel magnate or a congressman." After a brief "I'm glad to meet you," DiMaggio spent the evening demonstrating that he, like Marilyn, had no inclination for small talk. "I could see right away he was not a man to waste words," she wrote. "Acting mysterious and far away while in company was my own sort of specialty. I didn't see how it was going to work on somebody who was busy being mysterious and far away himself."

According to Marilyn, the only other dinner communication directed her way by DiMaggio was a shake of the head when she asked if it took him long to get the polka dot centered in his tie knot. Although attracted to this quiet man, Marilyn decided the date was a waste of time and made her excuses to leave, saying she had a hard day ahead at the studio for filming of *Don't Bother to Knock*. (This film was a failure, but it did give Marilyn the chance to show her abilities in a serious role, portraying a mentally ill babysitter.)

DiMaggio surprised Marilyn by standing up as she did. He walked her to her car, where he asked if she would give him a ride to his hotel. When they neared the hotel, DiMaggio suggested they take a drive, and Marilyn was glad to comply. Apparently, they drove around for three hours, occasionally breaking their contented silence with conversation. One point DiMaggio raised during the drive was how he always worried when he went out with a girl. "He didn't mind going out once with her," Marilyn wrote. "It was the second time he didn't like. As for the third time, that very seldom happened." But before the week was up, he would have survived his third dinner date with Marilyn, finding her an exception to his usual two-date rule.

Besides shattering Marilyn's previous perception of athletes as rowdy and flashy, DiMaggio overwhelmed her with his presence—or rather, the effect his presence had on everyone he encountered. During their blind-date dinner, Marilyn was fascinated by how DiMaggio was the center of attention rather than herself and noted how most of his admirers were men. "The men at the table weren't showing off for me or telling their stories for my attention," she wrote. "It was Mr. DiMaggio they were wooing. This was a novelty. No woman had ever put me so much in the shade before." By Hollywood standards, where the "big" men are those who talk longest and brag loudest, "my dinner companion was a nobody," Marilyn wrote. "Yet I had never met any man in Hollywood who got so much respect and attention at the dinner table."

In Don't Bother to Knock, *Marilyn was cast as a mentally ill babysitter with murderous intentions.*

Knowing that her new suitor was well respected, although she said she wasn't sure why, she contacted reporter James Bacon to get some publicity. "She said, 'I met the most wonderful man last night,'" Bacon recalled. "I said, 'Who was it?' She said, 'Joe DiMaggio.' I said, 'Joe DiMaggio! My God! He's the greatest baseball player since Babe Ruth.' She said, 'Oh, I didn't know that.' She didn't know how famous he was. She just thought he was a very nice guy."

Days after Marilyn's introduction to DiMaggio, she was the center of attention, but not because of any accomplishment. On April 28, production of her new film, *Monkey Business* (the last film on which she would be listed merely as a "costar") was halted, as Marilyn had to be admitted to Cedars of Lebanon Hospital for an appendectomy. In the operating room, surprised personnel found a note taped to the stomach of their not-yet blonde-all-over patient. (Soon afterward, she reportedly began bleaching her pubic hair.) The note read:

Most important to Read Before operation

Dear Doctor,

Cut as little as possible I know it seems vain but that doesn't really enter into it—the fact that I'm a *woman* is important and means much to me. You have children and you must know what it means—*please Doctor*—I know somehow you will! thank you—thank you—for Gods sakes Dear Doctor No *ovaries* removed—please again do whatever you can to prevent large *scars*. Thanking you with my all *heart*.

Marilyn Monroe

Although Marilyn had already terminated more than one pregnancy, conceivably causing great damage to her reproductive system because of the dangers inherent in illegally performed abortions, she was becoming increasingly obsessed with having a child. Her concerns were punctuated by the note episode, so a gynecologist was on hand during the surgery in the remote chance that any complications should arise. This onlooker, Dr. Leon Krohn, would later become Marilyn's doctor.

Marilyn's illness made headlines, reaffirming her great popularity, and DiMaggio was adding to her headline appeal with his increasing romantic interest in her. The surgeon who performed Marilyn's appendectomy said that calls streamed in from the former ball player, who was in New York, and that he sent roses by the dozen.

The Twentieth Century-Fox publicity department wasted no time in publicizing Marilyn's new relationship with "Joltin' Joe, the Yankee Clipper." DiMaggio visited Marilyn on the set of *Monkey Business*, and the studio promptly photographed them together, carefully cropping out Marilyn's costar, Cary Grant, who stood nearby. The studio had been awaiting the chance to photograph the two together ever since Marilyn mentioned her blind date with DiMaggio—particularly when she reported to work all smiles and laughter the next day.

Opposite: Marilyn's second-fiddle billing to Cary Grant in 1952's Monkey Business *was her last as mere costar. Right: Publicists captured a shot of Marilyn with her new and camera-shy beau, "Joltin' Joe," on the set of* Monkey Business, *and they carefully cropped out Grant from most of the released photographs.*

After six years in show business, Marilyn Monroe's transformation into a sex goddess was nearly complete, and she spent the rest of her life trying to move beyond that stereotype.

'out of wedlock' and never heard my illegal father's voice. I finally straightened these lies out, and I was surprised at the way the magazines and newspapers treated my 'new confessions.' They were kind and none of them picked on me."

Marilyn's business manager, Inez Melson, agreed to become conservator of Gladys' estate, in effect becoming her legal guardian. Gladys was soon moved to a private nursing home, Rockhaven Sanitarium, run by Agnes Richards, one of her old friends from her film-lab job. Marilyn visited her mother occasionally, but her main contribution to Gladys' life came in the way of financial support—an obligation that continued to be met by Marilyn's estate after her death ten years later. (Gladys lived almost another quarter century after her daughter's death, eventually succumbing to heart failure on March 11, 1984, in Gainesville, Florida.)

When the filming of *Monkey Business* wrapped up in late spring, the studio

As the Monroe-DiMaggio courtship began in early 1952, Marilyn was being forced to cope with her past. Until that year, Marilyn's mother, Gladys, had remained in an institution just outside of Los Angeles, with the state of California footing the bill. At this point, much of the biographical material Marilyn had supplied to interviewers and publicists came back to haunt her. She had passed herself off as an orphan, but disclosure by some journalists that her mother was indeed alive exposed her deceit, and the fact that Gladys was a ward of the state did not ease Marilyn's public embarrassment.

"I used to tell lies in my interviews—chiefly about my mother and father," Marilyn wrote years later. "I'd say she was dead—and he was somewhere in Europe. I lied because I was ashamed to have the world know my mother was in a mental institution—and that I had been born

executives at Twentieth Century-Fox finally decided that their blonde sensation should have a starring role. They could no longer ignore the impact she made upon the public. Fan mail had been pouring in—first as a trickle received back at Columbia after that studio abandoned Marilyn before *Ladies of the Chorus* opened in the theaters, then in a flood as her Twentieth Century-Fox string of films, most of them mediocre except for her presence, flashed across the screens. Her pile of fan mail far and away exceeded that of the studio's top star, Betty Grable. In her May 4, 1952 column, Hedda Hopper reflected on Marilyn's rise: "Blowtorch Blondes are Hollywood's specialty, and Marilyn Monroe who has zoomed to stardom after a three-year stretch as a cheesecake queen is easily the most delectable dish of the day…. Every producer at 20th is bidding for her as box office insurance."

*M*arilyn *on the set of* **Niagara.**

The setting for Marilyn's first starring role was Niagara Falls. As the star of *Niagara*, Marilyn portrayed an adulterous wife whose murderous plots bring about her own demise. The film made the most of her trademark breathy voice, but perhaps its most memorable highlight was a lengthy shot featuring Marilyn walking away from the camera, her swaying behind covered in a tight red dress.

Niagara required two weeks of location shooting at the Falls, so Marilyn stopped en route in New York City, where DiMaggio waited for her. She met his circle of close cronies—Toots Shor, a restaurateur and longtime friend, and George Solotaire, a Broadway ticket broker many years older than DiMaggio who soon came to think of Marilyn as a daughter. However, her first meeting with this group left her far short of impressed; irritated was a more accurate description of her frame of mind, since she had hoped to get a view of the city's arts centers rather than spend time with boisterous men. When she arrived at Niagara Falls for shooting, it became apparent that Marilyn was interested in a suitor other than Joe DiMaggio—one she had first dated six years before: Robert Slatzer.

Marilyn had called Slatzer in Ohio before she left Hollywood for New York to suggest he meet her at the *Niagara* location, and a studio publicist booked the journalist a room adjacent to Marilyn's at the General Brock Hotel. Slatzer said Marilyn was drinking heavily and lounging around nude, but the biggest shock of his visit was her pronouncement that Niagara Falls would be a "wonderful place to get married." Slatzer let the matter rest, since they had never discussed marriage and because Marilyn was fairly drunk when she brought up the subject. When he mentioned the possibility of marriage the next day, Marilyn balked.

Slatzer returned to Ohio to find he had lost his job as a result of his stay at Niagara Falls; when he told Marilyn what had happened, she suggested he return to her location. Before Slatzer's return, she paid DiMaggio another visit in New York, accompanied by her longtime makeup man and close friend, Whitey Snyder, one of the few people surrounding her of whom DiMaggio approved. Slatzer later arrived at Niagara Falls and then, at Marilyn's invitation, followed her back to Los Angeles when location shooting was finished.

Marilyn's love life in the summer of 1952 resembled a romantic comedy. She split her time and affections between Slatzer and DiMaggio. She juggled her evening schedules to accommodate whichever suitor was available, so as autumn approached Slatzer benefited when DiMaggio left town to broadcast the World Series. Inevitably, the two men met: Slatzer said that as he waited for Marilyn at her door, DiMaggio drove up, joined him in waiting outside the door, but said nothing. Marilyn let both men in, then argued with DiMaggio when "he was put out by the fact that I seemed to know the place pretty well," Slatzer said. DiMaggio asked Slatzer to leave, Slatzer refused, and Marilyn subsequently kicked them both out. "About an hour later she called and apologized, and said she'd gotten her schedules mixed up," Slatzer said.

The press was onto the story by late August, when columnist Dorothy Kilgallen ran the pronouncement: "A dark horse in the Marilyn Monroe romance derby is Bob Slatzer, former Columbus, Ohio, literary critic. He's

been wooing her by phone and mail, and improving her mind with gifts of the world's greatest books." Barely more than a month later, Slatzer says, he married Marilyn in Tijuana, Mexico, just across the California border, and they spent their wedding night, October 4, at the Rosarito Beach Hotel.

Before taking this huge step, Slatzer said, Marilyn had told him that she could never find happiness with DiMaggio, mainly because of his intense jealousy; even an autograph seeker would set him off. Slatzer and Marilyn had to decide "what we were going to do about DiMaggio," Slatzer said, "but Darryl Zanuck got to us first," insisting that the couple "get it undone." The three-day union ended when Slatzer and Marilyn returned to Tijuana and bribed the lawyer to destroy the marriage certificate before it could be filed.

Since Slatzer didn't acknowledge this marriage until long after Marilyn's death and because it somehow escaped exposure by the press, most people prefer to dismiss Slatzer's account. But biographer Summers found enough evidence to convince him of Slatzer's sincerity, including corroboration from various reputable sources who knew of the ill-fated union firsthand, including actress Terry Moore, former wife of Howard

For the second time in her career, this time in Niagara, murder was on the mind of Marilyn's character. Off-screen, however, according to Ohio journalist Robert Slatzer, her mind was on marriage—to him, not to Joe DiMaggio.

Hughes: "I think she was in a muddle over DiMaggio, and she liked Bob. She just ran into it and then ran out again." (Summers also found that Marilyn had begun an affair that spring that lasted close to a year with Nico Minardos, a Greek student-actor six years her junior, and said Marilyn talked of possible marriage to the young man more than once.)

Studio hostility toward Marilyn's marriage to Slatzer is easily justified. By the end of 1952, Twentieth Century-Fox declared Marilyn a full-fledged star, saying she was more publicized than Rita Hayworth or even the Queen of England. She had served as the first female Grand Marshal in the Miss America Parade in September, and even her dress, its neckline plunging almost to her waist, made headlines. Her volume of fan mail was up to five thousand letters a week. She had had a song written about her, and made her appearance at its garish, poolside ceremonial debut at the home of its singer, Ray Anthony, by stepping out of a helicopter that sent chairs and decorations flying with its rotary gusts. She had been a radio guest in November on the popular Edgar Bergen-Charlie McCarthy radio program. Marilyn also had begun shooting *Gentlemen Prefer Blondes* in late 1952, in which she shared top billing with Jane Russell. And she was finding a warmer spot in her heart for DiMaggio.

Sidney Skolsky said Marilyn left the studio's 1952 Christmas party to go home alone to her room at the Beverly Hills Hotel. She opened her door to find a miniature Christmas tree had been placed on the table, accompanied by a handwritten sign that read "Merry Christmas, Marilyn." In the corner of the room, to her delight, sat DiMaggio. A few days later, Marilyn confided to her friend Skolsky, "It's the first time in my life anyone ever gave me a Christmas tree. I was so happy I cried."

While DiMaggio was trying to win over Marilyn's heart that winter, Twentieth Century-Fox president Spyros Skouras was taking an interest in her increasing popularity and money-making potential. From his New York office, Skouras began instructing the studio executives to be more tolerant of their star. Thus began the pampering of Marilyn, who was already extremely prone to tardiness both on the set and off. Author Fred Guiles wrote of the studio's new attitude: "In one sense, this coddling had an adverse effect upon Marilyn's life: She needed the tension of opposition, for she had moved against contrary forces most of her life…. The crisis of her final summer had its beginnings in that winter of 1952–53 when Skouras began sending west his memos on how to keep Marilyn happy."

In November 1952, Marilyn shared the radio waves—and a special moment, it appears—with dummy Charlie McCarthy as Edgar Bergen's guest on **The Edgar Bergen and Charlie McCarthy Show.**

Chapter Three

A View From the Top

Hollywood's a place where they'll

pay you a thousand dollars for a kiss

and 50 cents for your soul.

I know, because I turned down

the first offer often enough

and held out for

the 50 cents.

After more than six years of struggle, Marilyn Monroe was finally recognized as a full-fledged star—even by Twentieth Century-Fox—as 1953 approached. There could have been no better way to start that year, a year during which she would achieve her greatest popular successes by Hollywood standards, than with a smash hit that seemed to have been tailored specifically to her talents.

Shooting on *Gentlemen Prefer Blondes*, the backdrop for Marilyn's unforgettable rendition of "Diamonds Are a Girl's Best Friend," began in November 1952. Many months before, as a twenty-sixth birthday present, Twentieth Century-Fox had told Marilyn that it was buying rights to the film for her. This fact was not made public knowledge, however, because the role of Lorelei Lee that would help cement Marilyn's stardom in 1953 seemed to be the exclusive property of another popular blonde, Carol Channing. Channing had originated the role on stage and played to standing-room-only crowds for months. Marilyn was advised to ignore columnists' speculation that Twentieth Century-Fox's purchase might provide Channing's film debut.

After filming began, Marilyn also ignored publicity concerning her "rivalry" with costar Jane Russell, with whom she shared top billing. Much to the studio publicists' dismay, Marilyn and Russell became close friends during filming, and this friendship lasted many years. The two women had been classmates at Van Nuys High School, where they had met at a school dance (in fact, they met while Marilyn was on one of her first dates with her former husband, Jim Dougherty). Also, both women were involved with sports figures—Marilyn was dating DiMaggio, and Russell was married to a former football player, Robert Waterfield. By suggesting that Marilyn enlist the

Much to Twentieth Century-Fox's dismay, there was no rivalry between Marilyn and Jane Russell on the set of **Gentlemen Prefer Blondes.**

aid of decorator Thomas Lane, Russell helped her put in order the three-room Beverly Hills apartment on Doheny Drive she rented in early 1953. Marilyn's contribution to the furnishings was the white piano her mother had bought her as a child, which she had succeeded in tracking down and purchasing.

Marilyn's tardiness remained a problem during the shooting of *Gentlemen*, but she managed to ease the resulting irritation by her hard work. Although she was earning less than a fifth of what Russell was paid, Marilyn was a perfectionist, sometimes demanding retakes even after the director was satisfied with the footage. (Marilyn was paid a maximum of $1,500 a week during the fourteen weeks of shooting [$18,000 in all], while Russell earned $100,000 or more.)

As filming wrapped up on *Gentlemen Prefer Blondes*, Marilyn's first starring vehicle, *Niagara*, premiered in February. Reviews were mixed, but the film cemented Marilyn's box office clout. She dominated the film, and her huge appeal also managed to quell any negative reaction to the way in which the film focused on her tightly clad bottom during a 116-foot (35m) walk, a daring piece of cinema for the early 1950s.

While *Niagara* made her studio realize its star's potential for major box office grosses, Marilyn was busy making another smash film, *How to Marry a Millionaire*—Twentieth Century-Fox's first feature film made for the wide screens of Cinemascope. A grueling filming schedule, in addition to the continued acting classes with Chekhov, made for a frenzied spring. As if her schedule wasn't hectic enough, she enrolled in the mime classes of director Lotte Goslar, whom she met after attending Goslar's staging of an Anton Chekhov play.

Marilyn stole the show from Lauren Bacall and Betty Grable in How to Marry a Millionaire, *but only after constant off-screen bolstering by her two protective costars.*

Marilyn attended the premiere of **How to Marry a Millionaire** *with Lauren Bacall and Humphrey Bogart, who pointed to Marilyn's frequent and time-consuming bathroom visits that night as a good reason not to drink excessively in a tight gown.*

Marilyn's whirlwind of activity that spring did not help her notorious tardiness. Again, and for the rest of her career, her lateness dragged out production time and wore on the nerves of all on the set, including her *How to Marry a Millionaire* costars Betty Grable, whom she had dethroned as queen of Twentieth Century-Fox, and Lauren Bacall. Grable and Bacall found themselves in the role of protectors, though, shielding Marilyn from excessive criticism and helping calm her bouts of extreme camera fright in the dressing room. Gable recognized Marilyn's emergence as her replacement and seemed to accept the inevitable with grace. Bacall, who was introduced to Marilyn by Johnny Hyde in 1950, was kind to Marilyn but tried to retain some distance because of her costar's "confused" personality.

Marilyn's performance in *How to Marry a Millionaire* was stunning. Her portrayal of the nearsighted Pola Debevoise may have been "the first time anybody genuinely liked Marilyn for herself in a picture," said Nunnally Johnson, the film's producer and screenwriter.

By the end of spring, and before the uproar over *Gentlemen Prefer Blondes* and *How to Marry a Millionaire*, Marilyn was off to the Canadian Rockies to shoot Otto Preminger's *River of No Return*, another Cinemascope movie. DiMaggio had planned to join her there so they could discuss their future—and the possibility of marriage—away from the Hollywood spotlights. Their relationship had endured more than a year, but the courtship had been anything but storybook: Marilyn still had not severed her ties to Nico Minardos and Robert Slatzer, and these were not her only affairs.

While DiMaggio was moving some of his suits into the new Doheny Drive apartment, biographer Summers reports, Marilyn was stepping out with two new lovers: dress designer Billy Travilla, whom she had known for three years, and Edward G. Robinson, Jr., son of the famous gangster portrayer and friend of her former lover Charlie Chaplin, Jr. Each affair lasted only a few weeks.

During one date, Travilla and Marilyn went to a club where Billie Holiday was performing. Before the show began, Travilla was on his way to the men's room when he noticed the "Miss Golden Dreams" calendar hanging on the wall of an open office. When he returned to the table and told Marilyn about the calendar, she asked that he take her to see it. The door to the office was now closed; Marilyn and Travilla knocked, told the man who opened the door that they had come to see the calendar, and then were surprised when Billie Holiday—who apparently was using the office as a dressing room and thinking they had come to visit her until she heard them inquire about the calendar—crumpled up the calendar and angrily threw it, along with a few choice profane words, at Marilyn. Travilla and Marilyn did not stay for the show.

As for Robinson, only nineteen at the time of his brief affair with Marilyn, passion soon gave way to friendship. But Robinson's bad habits may have had a more profound effect on Marilyn than their relationship. Arthur James, friend to both Chaplin and Robinson, referred to Robinson as a "pill freak." He told Summers, "We three men were a sort of trio, and Marilyn saw us all occasionally, together or separately, for the rest of her life. They were all depressives, Marilyn, Charlie and Eddie, and they would hunt each other down when things were bad…. But Charlie and Eddie were suicidal, more so than Marilyn. They couldn't make it on their own, and they couldn't deal with their famous names. Sometimes it was Marilyn who literally kept them alive." (Both barely outlived Marilyn: Chaplin died at forty-two, Robinson at forty.)

Marilyn admitted to being confused and unhappy, even though her career was taking off. Of her success in 1953, she wrote: "I had clothes, fame, money, a future, all the publicity I could dream of. I even had a few friends. And there was always a romance in the air. But instead of being happy over all these fairy-tale things that had happened to me I grew depressed and finally desperate. My life suddenly seemed as wrong and unbearable to me as it had in the days of my early despairs."

Before her twenty-seventh birthday, Marilyn accompanied DiMaggio to San Francisco for the funeral of his brother, Mike, who had drowned while fishing in Bodega Bay. The rumor mill heated up with talk of an impending marriage, even speculation that Marilyn and DiMaggio might already be married. Instead, when summer came, DiMaggio removed his clothes from the Doheny Drive apartment, much to the delight of Natasha Lytess, whose contempt for DiMaggio was overshadowed only by his extreme dislike for her.

Summer did bring one consolation for Marilyn: on June 26, 1953, she and her friend Jane Russell put their hands and feet into wet cement in front of Grauman's Chinese Theater to commemorate the premiere of *Gentlemen Prefer Blondes*. Marilyn dotted the "i" in her

Betty Grable graciously acceded to Marilyn her role as "queen" of Twentieth Century-Fox.

Marilyn and Jane Russell place their handprints in wet cement in front of Grauman's Chinese Theater in Hollywood on June 26, 1953, to mark the debut of Gentlemen Prefer Blondes. *The rhinestone Marilyn used to dot the "i" in her signature soon became the property of an enamored thief.*

name with a rhinestone; she had wanted a diamond to be used and also had suggested that she place her buttocks and Russell her bust in the cement, but her ideas were rejected. Reviews of the film were good, and it was a box office hit.

Back on the less-popular ground of reality, however, Marilyn left without DiMaggio to film *River of No Return*. Their planned getaway to talk of marriage seemed threatened, and she was not enthusiastic about making the movie.

Starring with Marilyn in *River* was Robert Mitchum. Mitchum had known of Marilyn when she was still calling herself Norma Jeane because he had worked alongside Jim Dougherty on a factory line during World War II. (Dougherty supposedly had shown Mitchum a nude photograph of his teenage wife.) Marilyn's sullen mood on location was vastly improved by Mitchum's antics, but director Preminger was a harder case to crack. He had trouble tolerating Marilyn's mistakes, and demanded that his stars perform rafting sequences that were normally left to stunt doubles. The result of his insistence was a couple of near accidents. Marilyn took advantage of the perilous conditions by claiming to injure her leg.

Shelley Winters, on location nearby for another movie, visited Marilyn on the set. After watching her struggle through a daylong shoot on a raft tied to the dock, Winters helped Marilyn ashore and told her to watch her step, warning that she could "break a leg on this slippery pier." This comment apparently inspired Marilyn: when her limousine arrived back at the hotel, she told Winters that she couldn't get out because she had broken her leg. Doctors arrived from Los Angeles the next day, after Marilyn assured Zanuck she could complete the picture despite her "considerable pain." X-rays revealed no damage, but Marilyn insisted that she needed a cast and crutches. The "injury" served to delay shooting, run up the budget, subdue Preminger, and bring DiMaggio running.

With cast and crutches for her "injured" leg, Marilyn and leading man Robert Mitchum barely muster smiles for the camera after the strenuous experiences, both on and off the set, during the filming of River of No Return.

DiMaggio brought along another doctor, his close friend George Solotaire, and plenty of outdoor gear for fishing excursions. DiMaggio's arrival perked up Marilyn considerably, but it further blackened the mood of Natasha Lytess. She already was upset over an argument with Marilyn involving Whitey Snyder, in which Lytess finally stated that he would have to leave or she would (Lytess remained with Marilyn for only two more films, while Snyder was around to prepare his friend's funeral makeup). She then had to tolerate having DiMaggio and Solotaire take up time with Marilyn that she and the star could have devoted to script rehearsal.

Lytess' irritability made her even more intolerable to Preminger on the set. Tommy Rettig, a ten-year-old actor who played Mitchum's son in the movie, was competent and a pleasure to direct throughout the film. One day he came to the set flustered and repeatedly blew his lines, finally breaking down when Marilyn tried to reassure him. (Marilyn was very fond of Rettig and had gone out of her way to win his confidence after he told her that a priest had warned him against socializing with "a woman like you.") Rettig's mother told Preminger that Lytess had upset the child the day before by telling him that all child actors lose their talents unless they take acting lessons; Tommy, too busy working to take classes, had been awake all that night fretting over Lytess' remarks.

Preminger reacted to this by barring Lytess from the set, both on location and at the studio. Marilyn said nothing during Preminger's tirade, but within two days he received a message from Zanuck asking that Lytess be allowed back on the set. Apparently Marilyn settled the argument by going straight to the studio head, for she believed Lytess to be vital to her career. From then on, Marilyn and Lytess spoke only in hushed whispers on the set.

Location shooting wrapped up, and the *River* cast boarded a train Preminger had chartered to take them home. En route to Los Angeles, Whitey Snyder asked Marilyn, "Why don't you marry that dago [DiMaggio] and raise a dozen kids?"

When Marilyn returned to Hollywood after filming River of No Return, she was determined to avoid another film debacle and refused to participate in an embarrassing saloon-girl project for Twentieth Century-Fox, leading to her suspension from the studio.

"Maybe I will," was her response. Conversations such as these, with Snyder encouraging Marilyn to give up her acting career in favor of a more stable lifestyle, pained Lytess. Although now head drama coach at Fox, she was not willing to have her most important pupil abandon her acting career.

Besides the tumultuous relationships during the shooting of *River of No Return*, dubbed "Picture of No Return" by leading man Mitchum because of its remote shoots and overruns, Marilyn had troubles to worry about back home. In September 1953, Grace McKee Goddard died from an overdose of barbiturates, an apparent suicide. Marilyn didn't know that Grace had died by her own hand; Doc Goddard was evasive about the cause of death, but Marilyn knew Grace had not been ill, and therefore assumed she had committed suicide. Marilyn made the funeral arrangements and had her "aunt" buried at Westwood Memorial Park.

Marilyn's personal and professional trials during the making of *River of No Return*, coupled with her likely awareness of how poor the movie and her performance were, must have made the prospect of marriage a welcome recourse. Having to make this all-wet Western added to Marilyn's discontent regarding the studio and may have played a large part in the decisions she made over the next few months.

Upon her return to Hollywood in September, Marilyn agreed to marry DiMaggio. "After much talk Joe and I had decided that since we couldn't give each other up, marriage was the only solution to our problem....We knew it wouldn't be an easy marriage." The wedding date was not determined, and they did not announce their engagement.

If the prospect of another marriage worried Marilyn, it didn't show when she made her television debut on September 13, 1953, on *The Jack Benny Show*. She played herself, the object of a dream fantasy for host Benny. About midway through the skit, Marilyn got the chance to take two years off her age, but that was nothing compared to Benny's trim job:

> BENNY: Marilyn. Marilyn—I know this is
> sudden, but will you...will you marry
> me?
> MARILYN: Marry? But, look at the difference
> in our ages!
> BENNY: Well, there isn't much difference,
> Marilyn. You're 25 and I'm 39.
> MARILYN: Yes, but what about 25 years from
> now, when I'm 50 and you're 39?
> BENNY: Gee, I never thought of that.

Television audiences finally got a small-screen glimpse of Marilyn on **The Jack Benny Show.**

Marilyn wore the 24-carat Moon of Baroda diamond, which dates to the fifteenth century, for the promotion of Gentlemen Prefer Blondes, the film that featured her signature performance of "Diamonds Are a Girl's Best Friend."

Later that month Marilyn attended a Hollywood party—alone, as she almost always did, as DiMaggio could barely tolerate Hollywood only slightly, and Hollywood parties not at all. The party host was Gene Kelly, and Marilyn spent much of the evening talking with Milton Greene, a New York photographer whose working honeymoon with his bride, Amy, brought him to Los Angeles on assignment for *Look* magazine. Marilyn and Greene had met at Twentieth Century-Fox earlier that week when he photographed her for *Look*'s Christmas issue.

While Amy Greene and Kelly's celebrity guests played charades, Marilyn and Milton Greene were setting the stage for a possible film-production partnership. This was the first of many meetings to come; Marilyn was open to the prospect of breaking free of her limiting contract with Twentieth Century-Fox, and Greene was willing to take whatever business risks were necessary—if he had some guarantee that Marilyn would follow through on her part. One of his concerns was whether she would continue acting if she married DiMaggio. This concern apparently was put to rest when, as she and DiMaggio publicly announced their plans to marry, Marilyn told reporters, "I intend to remain in pictures, but I'm looking forward to being a housewife too."

While looking ahead to the chance of greater artistic freedom and better earnings, Marilyn also paved the way for a possible singing career. In October she signed her first recording contract, with RCA Records, the former employer of one of her foster parents, Harvey Giffens. But she would never record an album for the label.

November brought the premiere of *How to Marry a Millionaire*, and the film was an overwhelming popular and critical success. Marilyn's performance proved that the comedic talents she displayed in *Gentlemen Prefer Blondes* were no fluke, and even the film's director, Jean Negulesco, admitted, "We did not know whether she'd been good or bad, and then when we put the picture together there was one person on that screen who was a great actress—Marilyn." Marilyn celebrated by getting drunk on the way to the premiere, accompanied by producer-scriptwriter Nunnally Johnson and his wife, as well as Humphrey Bogart and costar Lauren Bacall—her dates in the absence of publicity-shy DiMaggio.

Millionaire did wonders for Marilyn's image as a versatile actress. While *Gentlemen* had brought attention to her knack for comedy, she continued to play the typical dumb blonde. But behind the glasses of Pola in *Millionaire*, she displayed a sexuality and confidence that might otherwise have been lost behind the glitter of her more attractive roles. Her confidence was not trapped within her celluloid performance, however. Marilyn showed her studio how shrewd and stern she could be.

Just weeks after the near-debacle of *River of No Return*, Marilyn's studio informed her that her next movie project would be *The Girl in Pink Tights*. Her leading man would be her longtime idol, Frank Sinatra, and shooting would begin December 15. Her salary would be the usual maximum of $1,500 a week, while Sinatra would be paid $5,000 a week.

As the bespectacled Pola in **How to Marry a Millionaire,** *which debuted in November 1952, Marilyn won over critics and the public alike.*

"The title made me nervous," she wrote. "I was working with all my might trying to become an actress. I felt that the studio might cash in on exhibiting me in pink tights in a crude movie." Marilyn saw this film as the perfect platform for launching a battle for her rights. At issue, she said, was not her strained relationship with Zanuck or even the matter of getting more money. "The trouble was about something deeper," Marilyn wrote. "I wanted to be treated as a human being who had earned a few rights since her orphanage days." So in her first real act of defiance toward her studio, Marilyn balked when she was told to make *The Girl in Pink Tights*. (She made sure Sinatra knew her decision had nothing to do with him; she wanted to work with him.)

When the filming date arrived, Marilyn was nowhere to be found. Unknown to the studio, she had headed north to San Francisco to wait out the upcoming storm with DiMaggio, who hoped that the rift would be Marilyn's last bow as an actress. "I notified the studio that I couldn't agree to play in 'Pink Tights' until after I had read the script—and liked it…. The studio's first reply was to put me on suspension and take me off the payroll. I didn't mind. Their next move was to take me off suspension and put me back on salary. I didn't mind that either. Then a copy of 'The Girl in Pink Tights' script arrived. I read that and that I minded…. This dreary cliché-spouting bore in pink tights was the cheapest character I had ever read in a script." Marilyn's role was a schoolteacher-turned-saloon-showgirl who sacrificed her reputation to put her lover through college. In the end, she didn't even get the man for whom she labored. Instead, she married the saloon owner.

Even the studio's chosen director refused to shoot the film. "But that didn't help my case any," Marilyn wrote. "Everybody in the world could despise the picture, including, finally, the audience, and I would still remain in the wrong. This was because of my standing in the eyes of the front office. In these eyes I was still a sort of freak performer who had made good against its better judgment."

That Marilyn had "made good" was evident in 1953 not only by her ability to draw hordes to the box office, but also by the numerous accolades bestowed upon her: she was honored with the Golden Globe award for World Film Favorite, as well as named Fastest Rising Star by *Photoplay* magazine and Best Young Box Office Personality by *Redbook* magazine. Her successes of that year had been forecast by *Look* magazine when it named her Most Promising Female Newcomer in 1952. A young publisher named Hugh Hefner gambled his future on her popularity by purchasing (for a mere $500) one of Marilyn's nude photographs from the "Miss Golden Dreams" calendar for the feature photo spread in the first printing of *Playboy* magazine (December 1953). The *Playboy* cover displayed a more conservative pose than the feature spread, and the issue quickly sold out everywhere.

While Twentieth Century-Fox executives threatened to replace Marilyn in *The Girl in Pink Tights*, then suspended her just after the New Year (on January 4, 1954), their rebellious star and DiMaggio were making some drastic moves of their own. Marilyn

More than a year after the release of **How to Marry a Millionaire,** *Joe DiMaggio finally found out how to marry a sex goddess. Here the couple is all smiles as they wait for their courthouse ceremony in January 1954.*

wrote: "One day Joe said to me: 'You're having all this trouble with the studio and not working, so why don't we get married now? I've got to go to Japan anyway on some baseball business, and we could make a honeymoon out of the trip.' That's the way Joe is, always cool and practical."

On January 14, 1954, the wedding that the world had been expecting for almost two years finally took place. At San Francisco City Hall, Judge Charles Peery united a conservatively dressed Marilyn, clad in a brown

suit with a high ermine collar, and a glowing DiMaggio, dressed in the same blue-and-white tie he had worn on their first date for luck. Reno Barsochinni, manager of DiMaggio's restaurant on Fisherman's Wharf, served as best man, and on hand were about a dozen guests, including DiMaggio's family and best friends, George Solotaire and former Yankee pitcher and Pacific League manager Lefty O'Doul. Marilyn's friends were conspicuously absent.

The wedding was not the most organized affair: Judge Peery was interrupted at a Bar Association lunch by a telephone call from Barsochinni, who asked that he perform the civil ceremony as soon as possible. But Marilyn made sure that she took time out before her wedding to phone the publicity director at the studio and some of her preferred press contacts. By the time the judge was ready to begin, hundreds had gathered outside City Hall, and the hallways were jammed with reporters. Just as she had during her appearance on *The Jack Benny Show*, Marilyn shaved a few years off her age (she said she was twenty-five) when she signed her marriage certificate as Norma Jeane Mortensen Dougherty. She then promised to "love, honor, and cherish" DiMaggio; the traditional tenet "obey" was not included, although the omission of "obey" was becoming standard practice at the time.

Rather than a shower of rice, the newlyweds were met with a barrage of reporters' questions following the ceremony. After Marilyn pronounced that they would have six children, DiMaggio drove away with his bride in his blue Cadillac. The couple drove two hundred miles (320km) south for a candlelit steak dinner at Paso Robles. From there they doubled back to the Clifton Hotel, hung out a "Do Not Disturb" sign, and settled in for fifteen hours. After that, reporters lost the couple's trail—supposedly Marilyn and Joe had headed east to a friend's mountain cabin near Palm Springs. There, without a television set around to distract DiMaggio (his obsessive television viewing always irritated and alienated Marilyn), the DiMaggios spent two weeks of marital bliss, taking walks in the snow and playing billiards.

Marilyn's marriage to DiMaggio intensified the already-bright spotlight that followed her. Her studio, realizing that she was bigger than Twentieth Century-Fox itself, reinstated her—and ate some humble pie to lure her back. Marilyn, well represented while she was away by her attorneys and agent, had won her fight—the temporary settlement put *Pink Tights* on hold and gave Marilyn a salary increase. Yet the war, it turns out, had barely begun.

A kiss seals the deal for the DiMaggios in the office of San Francisco Municipal Judge Charles S. Peery.

After a brief stay at the DiMaggio family's San Francisco home, in February 1954 Marilyn and DiMaggio set out with Lefty O'Doul and his wife, Jean, for Tokyo, where "The Slugger" was to embark on a promotional tour pitching the opening of baseball season in Japan. The trip was a spectacle from the very beginning. When the couple's plane refueled in

A month after they were married, Marilyn and DiMaggio embarked on their "honeymoon" trip to Japan, stopping over in Hawaii on the way—just long enough to be mobbed by fans and media.

Hawaii, thousands of fans were waiting; as they made their way to the airport lounge to wait while the plane was readied, fans swarmed around Marilyn. But this was nothing compared to their Tokyo reception. To escape the hysterical crowds chanting *monchan* (precious little girl), the DiMaggios were deplaned through a baggage hatch. The mobs grabbed at Marilyn, pulling her hair. She hid her panic very well, but later told Sidney Skolsky that she felt "like some dictator in a wartime newsreel."

Over the next ten days, the star-struck Japanese calmed down somewhat, and Marilyn settled into the role of Mrs. DiMaggio. While her husband made the promotional rounds, Marilyn and Jean O'Doul prepared for another type of tour: Marilyn was headed to Korea to entertain the U.S. troops, and Jean agreed to accompany her. Details vary as to how the tour was arranged. According to Marilyn, the trip was proposed by an Army officer who had been on their plane to Japan. Biographer Fred Guiles wrote that Marilyn was asked to tour by a high-ranking officer whom she and DiMaggio met at a cocktail party more than a week after arriving in Tokyo. Others contend that Marilyn had planned the tour before she ever left America, and that DiMaggio consented grudgingly.

The first of ten shows over a four-day period took place February 16. Marilyn wrote that the tour started at "a hospital full of wounded soldiers." She immediately hit a snag when a conservative officer insisted that she change the Gershwin song "Do It Again" to "Kiss Me Again" because of "lewd" lyrics. Then she said they left for the front to entertain the Forty-Fifth Division. "It was cold and starting to snow," Marilyn wrote. "I was backstage in dungarees." But when told that the men were getting restless and starting to throw rocks on the stage, "I changed into my silk gown as quickly as I could. It had a low neckline and no sleeves. I felt worried all of a sudden about my material, not the Gershwin song but the others I was going to sing— 'Diamonds Are a Girl's Best Friend.' It seemed like the wrong thing to say to soldiers in Korea, earning only soldiers' pay. Then I remembered the dance I did after the song. It was a cute dance. I knew they would like it."

Marilyn's sacrifices—donning revealing gowns and open-toed shoes, even amid swirling snow, while thirteen thousand lustful GIs sat bundled in thick coats and gloves— revealed a great deal about her feelings for the troops. She believed that soldiers were responsible for her star status: "I became famous in the movies…entirely at the insistence of the movie public, and most of this movie public was in uniform in Korea, fighting," she wrote in *My Story*. For her

Left: This 1951 photograph established Marilyn as a favorite pinup girl among soldiers in World War II. One U.S. Army regiment stationed in Korea named her the "Girl We'd Most Like to Chogie Up With" ("Chogie" means "climb" in Korean). *Above and opposite, right:* Marilyn wows the troops in Korea, 1954. *Opposite, left:* Marilyn gets friendly with a couple of the boys.

To the Japanese press:

Q:

How long have you been walking
that way?

M:

I started when I was 6 months old
and haven't stopped yet.

efforts, she was rewarded with a mild case of pneumonia upon her return to Tokyo. Still, Marilyn would forever consider the Korea trip the most successful and satisfying moment of her entire career. "It was the first time that I ever felt I had an effect on people," she said. And she had told the Army contingent as she left Korea, "This was the best thing that ever happened to me. I only wish I could have seen more of the boys, all of them."

Four days of rest and antibiotics back in Tokyo brought the fever caused by her mild illness under control so that she and DiMaggio could continue to tour Japan. From Japan they returned to San Francisco, where she was embraced, but not with a mob mentality. Marilyn found much solace there, as San Franciscans respected her privacy and that of her husband. Soon, however, she and DiMaggio began to quarrel. As they settled into their married life, the tolerance and patience they exhibited in their courtship and first few weeks of their marriage began to erode.

Marilyn returned to Hollywood amid much fanfare in late March to be honored as Best Actress by *Photoplay* magazine for her work in *Gentlemen Prefer Blondes* and *How to Marry a Millionaire*; DiMaggio, true to form, did not accompany her to the awards presentation (he told her he would attend such a ceremony only if she were nominated to win an Academy Award). She also set about patching up her relations with Twentieth Century-Fox, even as she intensified her business talks with future partner Milton Greene. To show her dedication to the uneasy truce with Twentieth Century-Fox, Marilyn agreed to star in a tribute to Irving Berlin, *There's No Business Like Show Business*, apparently because they had promised her a more desirable vehicle, the Broadway hit *The Seven Year Itch*. The weak script of *There's No Business Like Show Business* made *The Girl in Pink Tights* look respectable, although this wasn't saying much.

Marilyn also demonstrated her loyalty to Hollywood by convincing DiMaggio to rent an eight-room, two-story Beverly Hills cottage. The house, just a stone's throw from bustling San Vicente Avenue, was not the best choice for the DiMaggios, as it was highly accessible—its front door opened almost onto the sidewalk—and its previous tenants had left the house a mess. The kitchen was so filthy that Marilyn despaired, "It must be full of germs. It will be terrible for Joe's ulcers!"

Work on *There's No Business Like Show Business* began the Monday after the DiMaggios moved into the house, and it was soon apparent that problems at home were affecting her work on the set. One of the few bright spots was her sizzling rendition of "Heat Wave," in which she was decked out like a blonde Carmen Miranda, but without the fruit on her head; even this performance was panned by many critics. (Because of her RCA contract, Marilyn's singing performances were not included on the film's soundtrack album.) Although Marilyn's studio had hoped that DiMaggio would help them feed the public's insatiable appetite for Marilyn-related tidbits, he showed up on the set only once

Even Marilyn's stunning appearance couldn't dress up the garish Irving Berlin tribute **There's No Business Like Show Business.**

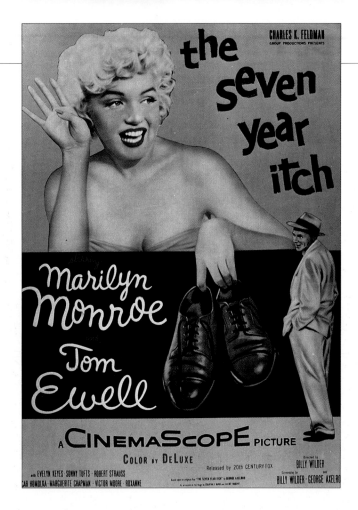

and refused to pose with Marilyn because of her skimpy outfit, preferring to be photographed instead with Marilyn's costar Ethel Merman and the musical genius to whom the film was dedicated, Irving Berlin.

When production was wrapped up in August, Marilyn moved immediately into filming *The Seven Year Itch*, produced, directed, and cowritten by Billy Wilder. Rumors were spreading that her marriage to DiMaggio was on its last legs, but upon her arrival in New York on September 9 for location shooting, she assured the press that all was well between them and that "a happy marriage comes before anything." Two days after Marilyn's arrival, DiMaggio joined her at her hotel, although Marilyn feared at first that her husband was on hand as a chaperone rather than companion. But less than a week later, on September 15, Marilyn's infamous skirt-blowing spectacle proved to be the straw that broke the back of the DiMaggios' failing marriage.

The filming of this celebrated scene drew about four thousand spectators to the Trans-Lux Theatre, on the corner of Fifty-second Street and

While The Seven Year Itch should have been a cause of celebration for Marilyn, who savored her role in the film, the experience was overshadowed by her eroding eight-month marriage to DiMaggio, who lost his cool over the infamous skirt-blowing scene.

Lexington Avenue, even though it took place in the middle of the night. DiMaggio had avoided production sites since his arrival, but while out drinking with George Solotaire and Walter Winchell, was convinced by Winchell to check out the action. Seeing a mob of thousands enjoying the sight of his wife's white, backless dress repeatedly being blown above her head to reveal her white panties as she stood over a subway grating (a wind machine was being operated below), DiMaggio muttered, "What the hell's going on here?" Louder, he said to Winchell, "I told you I never did this. Let's get out of here."

The arguments that followed between Marilyn and an enraged DiMaggio when they returned separately to the St. Regis Hotel around 4 A.M. kept some crew members awake in neighboring rooms. Biographer Summers reports that Milton Greene's wife, Amy, saw bruises on Marilyn's back the next day, but these were concealed by her wardrobe and makeup crew so that she could complete filming. (Amy had accompanied her husband to New York to visit Marilyn. Greene had hired two attorneys and an accountant, and was ready to legally put the Greene-Monroe business conspiracy into motion.) DiMaggio already had flown back to Los Angeles.

The day after the skirt scene, when Greene brought to Marilyn's suite some papers for her to go over, his soon-to-be partner was in no condition to comprehend legalese. She had been drinking champagne to excess and now, with the aid of sedatives, apparently had reached a stuporlike state. Greene soon found out why: her marriage to DiMaggio was over.

Marilyn returned to her Beverly Hills home and contacted lawyer Jerry Giesler to set her divorce from DiMaggio in motion. The day the couple announced their legal separation, Marilyn called Wilder to tell him she wouldn't be able to work. DiMaggio packed his belongings as Marilyn repeatedly made up her tear-streaked face upstairs. Marilyn's business agent, Inez Melson, was on hand to answer phone calls and turn away reporters. DiMaggio was the first to face the hordes of reporters and bystanders outside, where his friend Reno Barsochinni waited to take him back to San Francisco. When asked by reporters if he would be returning to Los Angeles, DiMaggio replied, "San Francisco's my home. It's always been my home. I'll never be coming back to this house."

Almost an hour after DiMaggio's departure, dressed in black and physically supported by her lawyer and Twentieth Century-Fox publicity director Harry Brand, Marilyn left the house; she could only stutter and sob when reporters fired

A tearful Marilyn faces nearly a hundred reporters on October 6, 1954, shortly after DiMaggio drove away from their Beverly Hills home for the last time.

their questions. Billy Travilla told Anthony Summers that he found out later she had more than her divorce to worry about: "On Marilyn's way to the car someone gave her an envelope with a piece of toilet paper inside. The word *whore* was written on it in fecal matter.... The people in front of the house were his fans, not hers." The trauma of announcing her divorce would turn to apparent relief within hours, however; she returned to the set of *The Seven Year Itch* with a competence and enthusiasm for work that surprised and delighted Wilder.

Close to the end of the film, Wilder was preparing for the worst when it came time to shoot a scene involving a long speech by Marilyn. Wilder expected the scene to take several days, but "three minutes later, it was all over," said George Axelrod, author of both the original play and the screenplay for *The Seven Year Itch*. "Marilyn had done it, letter perfect and with an emotional impact that caused the entire soundstage to burst into applause at the end, on the first take. There was no need for a second. She told me later she was able to do the scene because she believed every word of what she was saying and because it seemed to her like the story of her own life." The speech referred to Marilyn's definite attraction to rather quiet men whose physical attributes wouldn't earn them a second look but whose underlying tenderness and strength of character showed through and excited her.

By November 4, one week after authorities granted her divorce from DiMaggio, filming was complete. The completion of *The Seven Year Itch* not only marked the end of her brief marriage, it signaled the end of an equally stormy but much longer relationship with Twentieth Century-Fox

M̳arilyn waiting to testify in her divorce action against DiMaggio.

and Hollywood itself. Marilyn already was plotting a major declaration of independence—her escape from the studio and from private investigators hired by DiMaggio who had been shadowing her for up to six months.

A few days after DiMaggio left the Beverly Hills home as his formal separation from Marilyn began—perhaps even months before then—he enlisted the aid of a private detective, Barney Ruditsky, to keep an eye on his estranged wife. Marilyn had been holed up at the studio during the last weeks of filming, refusing to see DiMaggio, and he had been barred from the studio lot by Darryl Zanuck. Although hoping for a reconciliation, DiMaggio did not appear for the divorce hearing on October 27 at Santa Monica Courthouse. Marilyn was granted her freedom on the grounds of "mental cruelty" after telling the judge that their "relationship was mostly one of coldness and indifference." She said DiMaggio would refuse to talk to her for a week at a time or longer and permitted her no visitors. Apparently, about the only thing she had no complaints about was their sexual relationship. She later told author Truman Capote that if satisfying sex was "all it takes, we'd still be married." Even though Marilyn's divorce petition had been granted, she legally remained DiMaggio's wife until the decree was finalized almost a year later.

Despite his absence during the divorce hearing, DiMaggio surprised the press by contacting them to reveal that he wanted to be reconciled and said, "I hope she'll see the light." DiMaggio seemed convinced that Marilyn sought a divorce because she was involved with another man. His prime suspect was Hal Schaefer, Marilyn's voice coach for both *Gentlemen Prefer Blondes* and *There's No Business Like Show Business*. Schaefer acknowledged that he and Marilyn had a brief affair that began just months after she married DiMaggio. Schaefer also said that she was being followed by private investigators before the summer, and he suspected that her car had been bugged.

Despondence over work and depression compounded by his feelings for Mrs. DiMaggio led Schaefer to attempt suicide in late July. He barely survived. During his long recuperation, Schaefer said, Marilyn often visited him in the hospital and at his beach home to help nurse him to health; she was followed each time. When he recovered enough to return to work and during her divorce ordeal, he said, they would meet secretly to avoid scandal. But their efforts—and their relationship—ended after an embarrassing spectacle that came to be known as the "Wrong Door Raid."

On November 5, the day after being granted her divorce from DiMaggio, Marilyn was invited for a late dinner at the Hollywood apartment of actress Sheila Stewart, to which Schaefer accompanied her. Outside, Philip Irwin, a private detective who said he had been following Marilyn for several months under the direction of private investigator Ruditsky, spotted Marilyn's car parked outside the apartment and phoned his boss. Ruditsky joined Irwin at the stakeout to verify that Marilyn was indeed there. He then placed a call to the Villa Capri, reportedly the site of Marilyn's first date with DiMaggio, where DiMaggio was spending an evening with Frank Sinatra.

At the Villa Capri, Sinatra received the phone call from Ruditsky. Reporter Jim Bacon also was in the restaurant, and he watched as Sinatra talked animatedly with his companions, who included DiMaggio and Sammy Davis, Jr. Sinatra and DiMaggio had become close friends, and they shared the aggravation of failure at marriage; Sinatra had been through a turbulent and sometimes violent relationship with his latest wife, Ava Gardner. Bacon said Sinatra and DiMaggio argued and then left the restaurant in separate cars.

Irwin said DiMaggio was the first to arrive at the apartment building on the corner of Kilkea Drive and Waring Avenue, and also said that the athlete circled the block twice before parking behind Marilyn's car. He started walking toward the apartment but was stopped by Irwin; Sinatra drove up soon afterward. Virginia Blasgen, owner of the apartment com-

plex, saw the two men outside around 10 P.M. She said DiMaggio was "mad, and was walking up and down," while Sinatra "was jumping up and down and grinning at me." But being spotted did not deter them; they apparently were convinced they would catch Marilyn with "the other man."

At 11:15 P.M., Florence Kotz awoke to the frightening crash of her door being broken down and the glare of camera-bulb flashes. She screamed, and the intruders scrambled in retreat. DiMaggio and his bungling entourage had broken into the wrong apartment. Upstairs, Marilyn and company heard the crash of Kotz's door. Suspecting that the break-in had something to do with her being at the apartment, Marilyn headed home. Another detective on the team that had Marilyn under surveillance said DiMaggio showed up at Marilyn's house just two hours after the "Wrong Door Raid," and had not left when the detective ended his vigil outside.

The identity of the intruders would not be known for another two years, when an article in *Confidential* magazine revealed enough information to bring about probes by a state Senate committee and a Los Angeles grand jury. When called to testify, Sinatra claimed he had stayed in the car while DiMaggio, Irwin, and Ruditsky broke into Kotz's apartment; Irwin countered that Sinatra indeed was an active participant; and DiMaggio avoided testifying altogether by leaving the state during the proceedings. The only justice from the whole ordeal was the settlement of $7,500 granted to Kotz (in the two years since the break-in she had married, and her last name now was Ross), who had sued DiMaggio, Sinatra, and others connected to the break-in when their participation was revealed. With the accused parties giving conflicting testimony, the investigation, though unresolved, finally was laid to rest.

In the meantime, as baffled police classified what had happened at Kotz's apartment as an attempted burglary, Marilyn was feted by Hollywood's elite to celebrate completion of *The Seven Year Itch*. Her agent, Charles Feldman, coproducer of *Itch*, brought together eighty of the film industry's most prominent players, including Marilyn's lifelong idol, Clark Gable. The party was held at Romanoff's restaurant, an exclusive watering hole for the stars. Johnny Hyde had taken Marilyn there during his campaign to make her a star, and had even had his home decorated to resemble the restaurant, complete with white booths and a dance floor. Now Marilyn was the guest of honor, yet she was an hour late arriving, although not through any fault of her own.

Photographer Sam Shaw, a friend to Marilyn since their first meeting in 1951 or 1952, was her escort for the evening. (He had been hired by Twentieth Century-Fox to shoot publicity stills of Marilyn for *The Seven Year Itch*.) On the way to the party, their car ran out of gasoline. Although dressed to kill, neither Marilyn nor Shaw had any money, so Marilyn "sweet-talked a gas attendant for gas," Shaw said.

Upon her arrival, Marilyn felt "like Cinderella," amazed that so many important people would show up in her honor. Marilyn remained at her party until 3 A.M., and her amazement never wavered throughout the evening. She fulfilled her fantasy of meeting Gable, and she asked him for his autograph. They danced together and even discussed the possibility of costarring in a film.

The day after the party, Marilyn was driven to Cedars of Lebanon Hospital by DiMaggio after she complained of being sick to her stomach on November 6. She underwent surgery, reportedly to correct a chronic gynecological problem, and DiMaggio, vigilant in his hopes for a reconciliation, stayed by her side at the hospital. She left the hospital after four days, and was seen dining with DiMaggio at the Villa Capri on the night of her release. Reporters again speculated that the couple might get back together, but reconciliation was the furthest thing from Marilyn's mind—whether with DiMaggio or with the studio that helped push her toward matrimony in the first place.

Marilyn finally found something to smile about in 1955, when she turned her back on Hollywood to form her own production company in New York.

Modeled After Marilyn:
Her Imitators

While she was accustomed to adulation, even Marilyn Monroe might have blushed at the outpouring of women—and men—who try to capture her wiggle, whisper, and other delightfully wanton mannerisms in look-alike contests held around the world.

Whether vying for rewards of cash prizes or a career boost, many contestants take their efforts very, very seriously. Some will travel thousands of miles for the chance to be heralded most like Marilyn, because even over three decades after her death, her style and semblance are highly marketable assets. For some, these contests launch prosperous careers as doubles; these people can earn thousands of dollars annually just for appearing at mall openings or in advertisements as "Marilyn."

At a look-alike contest at Mann's (previously Grauman's) Chinese Theater in Hollywood, held a couple of days before what would have been Marilyn's sixty-fifth birthday, the half dozen finalists included two men who might have made even DiMaggio look twice. Nonetheless, the winner was a woman—the youngest-looking impostor on hand, partly because some of the contestants of starlet age became scarce after learning they had confused the contest with a simultaneously occurring audition for a television film about Marilyn.

Brit Kay Kent modeled her life—and her death—after Marilyn's. In this October 1988 photograph, Kent wears a gold lurex pantsuit of Marilyn's that was slated for auction at Christie's of London that year.

For the most part, Marilyn imitators inject a lot of fun into their mimicry, but as with just about anything, there are those who take their identification with Marilyn to the extreme—such as Kay Kent, the twenty-

five-year-old professional Marilyn double in England who, in the summer of 1989 after her boyfriend left her, took her life with the help of sleeping pills and a half bottle of vodka. The platinum blonde's nude body was found sprawled across her bed. She had said at one point in her high-paying career as "Marilyn" (she earned around $90,000 the year before her suicide), "It's almost as though by taking on her appearance I've inherited her troubles."

Fortunately, such extreme affiliations with Marilyn are the exception rather than the norm. The better-rounded of the imitators shed the "Marilyn" persona once they leave the stage, just as the real Marilyn usually did, according to her closest friends. They marveled at how she could transform herself instantly from just another face in the crowd to one that drew mobs when she "just felt like being Marilyn for a while."

Forty-three Marilyn look-alikes were on hand in 1990 to promote the annual Castroville, California, Artichoke Festival, where forty-three years earlier Marilyn had become the first California Artichoke Queen.

Chapter Four

To New York and a New Life

I'm trying to prove to myself

that I'm a real person.

Then maybe I'll convince myself

that I'm an actress.

How to Be Very, Very Popular was selected by Twentieth Century-Fox as Marilyn's next film. Nunnally Johnson, screenplay writer for *How to Marry a Millionaire*, penned the new script specifically for her. But when shooting was to begin on January 15, 1955, Marilyn was not on the studio set; she was not even on the West Coast. For she had declared herself "no longer contractually bound to Twentieth Century-Fox" after the completion of *The Seven Year Itch*.

Just before Christmas 1954, Marilyn turned her back on the Hollywood that was finally embracing her. She boarded a plane under the alias Zelda Zonk and headed for New York, home base for her planned enterprise: Marilyn Monroe Productions. Also on the plane was Milton Greene, who was to run the production business and handle all finances. The fruit of his efforts over the past year in making the venture a reality would be 49.5 of the firm's 101 shares, with Marilyn holding the other 51.5. Earlier in the year, Greene's lawyers had determined Marilyn's contract with Twentieth Century-Fox to be invalid on the grounds that it amounted to "slave labor" and that the studio had "neglected" to tell her formally that their agreement was being renewed.

Prospects of creative independence and greater earnings gave Marilyn the confidence to leave behind Hollywood, where she had struggled, to forge a whole new existence in New York. Greene demonstrated his confidence in Marilyn and their venture by leaving his $50,000-a-year job with *Look* to devote all his attention to Marilyn Monroe Productions.

Marilyn with business partner Milton Greene (left), the driving force behind Marilyn Monroe Productions, and studio mogul Jack Warner.

After a short stay at The Gladstone Hotel in New York while her partnership with Greene was worked out, Marilyn moved to the Greenes' country home in Weston, Connecticut. As Christmas approached, the Greenes fielded a stream of calls from famous people who were trying to track down the missing star, including Bob Hope, who hoped to persuade Marilyn to do his Korea Christmas show for the U.S. troops.

On December 31, 1954—just before Marilyn babysat the Greenes' year-old son, Joshua, so that they could attend a New Year's Eve party—Marilyn Monroe Productions was formalized. The partnership was announced at a press conference on January 7, 1955, at the Manhattan home of attorney Frank Delaney. Responding to a somewhat hostile press, Marilyn said she was toning down her platinum look, broadening her "scope," and taking charge of her career "so I can play the better kind of roles I want to play." She added that she was "tired of sex roles" and preferred dramatic vehicles such as *The Brothers Karamazov* by Dostoyevsky. "I don't want to play the brothers," she said. "I want to play Grushenka. She's a girl."

When Marilyn failed to show up on the set for production of *How to Be Very, Very Popular*—a year and a week after her suspension for refusing to star in *The Girl in Pink Tights*—she was suspended once again by Twentieth Century-Fox.

Tranquillity at the Greenes' twenty-five-acre (10ha) Connecticut farm probably pushed many of the nightmarish events of the past year far from Marilyn's mind. She enjoyed drives with Amy through the snow-covered landscape—often putting the top down on the convertible and turning up the heat. She went for long walks, and from the studio she inhabited, separate from the Greenes' eighteenth-century farmhouse, she could stand on the balcony and look out over the farm's lake. She went on shopping sprees (financed by Greene) with Amy in Manhattan, ben-

efiting from the taste and sense of style of her friend, who later became fashion editor for *Glamour* magazine. She also benefited from Amy's graceful self-confidence, which seemed to rub off on Marilyn.

With the arrival of spring, Marilyn began to spend more and more time in New York City, and the bustling metropolis seemed to stimulate her. While she was quite nervous when she had to deliver dialogue before a camera, she could muster up a fairly gruff impatience, especially when dealing with taxi drivers, on the streets of New York. But she was gracious and tolerant with her fans in the city, who included a fanatical group of teenagers who would wait hours just for a glimpse of her. One especially devout group, all under the age of nineteen, were so resolute in their idolization that they became known as the Monroe Six. Just as persistent was a sixteen-year-old loner, James Haspiel, who had first met Marilyn and talked her into a kiss the year before when she was shooting the infamous skirt scene for *The Seven Year Itch*. These young people, especially Haspiel, came to mean a great deal to Marilyn.

Making friends came easily to Marilyn in New York, and among the most cherished and long-lasting friendships she enjoyed was with poet Norman Rosten and his wife, Hedda. In early 1955, photographer Sam Shaw and Marilyn were on an outing in the City, when they were caught suddenly in a torrential downpour. Realizing they were near the apartment of his good friend Rosten, Shaw called to ask whether he and his companion could drop in to wait out the rain. Shaw arrived with Marilyn at Rosten's door and apparently mumbled an introduction. When she had taken off her wet coat, Marilyn was drawn to the Rostens' enormous bookcase, reached for a volume that caught her eye, and began to read—a collection of poems written by Rosten for his daughter, Patricia. The Rostens still had no idea who their quiet guest was, and when Hedda asked her what she did for a living, she surprised them by explaining that she was Marilyn Monroe.

When announcing Marilyn Monroe Productions:

Q:

We heard there's something new about you. What is it?

M:

Well, my hair is new. I used to be platinum.... Now I'm a subdued platinum; not as loud as the other.

Lee and Paula Strasberg's influence intensified Marilyn's determination to be taken seriously as an actress.

The Rostens gave Marilyn the book of poetry that had so enthralled her. A few days later, Marilyn wrote a note of thanks to her hospitable hosts, telling them how the poetry had softened her stance about wanting only a son and expressed her desire to see them again. Soon afterward the Rostens began to invite her to informal poetry readings and dinners at their home. It was at one of these dinners in March that Marilyn met Cheryl Crawford, who cofounded the famed Actors Studio in 1947 with Elia Kazan and Robert Lewis.

When Marilyn expressed to Crawford her determination to become a serious actress, she was invited to visit the Actors Studio and meet its artistic director, Lee Strasberg. Later that week, Marilyn had her first pri-

vate lesson with Strasberg in his apartment on Central Park West. These lessons increased to twice weekly and finally prepared her to join the studio class. Although she never became an official member of the Actors Studio, an honor reserved for actors with stage experience, she did become one of its most celebrated pupils, alongside luminaries like Marlon Brando and James Dean.

Lee Strasberg and his wife, Paula, quickly became two of the most influential people in Marilyn's life. As masters of "The Method," they encouraged their students to look inward and to past personal experiences for motivation and understanding of a character. Thus Marilyn was reintroduced to the benefits of psychoanalysis to heighten self-awareness. She had undergone therapy for about six months in Hollywood during her marriage to DiMaggio; in New York she became heavily dependent on the doctor Milton Greene had found for her and visited the analyst's office up to five times a week as long-buried emotions began to be exposed. Marilyn also found that psychoanalysis helped her control the quick temper she apparently had inherited from her grandmother, Della. Marilyn also became increasingly dependent on the Strasbergs, who offered encouragement and guidance based on their zealous faith in her great acting potential. Lee Strasberg said of Marilyn in 1956, "I have worked with hundreds and hundreds of actors and actresses, and there are only two that stand out above the rest. Number one is Marlon Brando, and the second is Marilyn Monroe."

Still, Marilyn could see that the Strasbergs were not the only worthy mentors. She met and befriended author Truman Capote at El Morocco, the prestigious New York nightclub in which she had met her friend Henry Rosenfeld in 1949. Capote introduced her to actress Constance Collier, by then a famous acting coach. (Collier, perhaps best remembered by audiences for her performance in the 1937 film *Stage Door*, had coached actresses Audrey Hepburn, Katharine Hepburn, and Vivien Leigh, among others.) Marilyn began to take instruction from Collier, but her teacher died after only a few weeks of instruction, at the age of seventy-seven.

Before her death, Collier offered the following appraisal of Marilyn's potential, which contradicted the Strasbergs' view regarding her stage talents: "I don't think she's an actress at all, not in any traditional sense. What she has—this presence, this luminosity, this flickering intelligence—could never surface on the stage. It's so fragile and subtle, it can only be caught by the camera. It's like a hummingbird in flight; only a camera can freeze the poetry of it. But anyone who thinks this girl is simply another Harlow, or harlot or whatever, is mad. I hope, I really pray, that she survives long enough to free the strange lovely talent that's wandering through her like a jailed spirit."

Marilyn's luminosity certainly bolstered her film career, and it also made some powerful people consider her suitability for a royal title. Tycoon Aristotle Onassis had gotten out the word that Prince Rainier of Monaco was seeking a bride—one with enough popular international appeal to revive interest in visiting his tiny principality. Contacted by Onassis' friend George Schlee, *Look* publisher Gardner Cowles (a neighbor of the Greenes) suggested that Marilyn be approached with the royal proposition. She said she'd be happy to meet "Prince Reindeer," but the prince put an end to that idea by announcing his engagement to actress Grace Kelly. Marilyn responded to the news by calling the future princess with her congratulations, adding, "I'm so glad you've found a way out of this business."

Although she rarely smoked, Marilyn accepts a light from Edward R. Murrow to try to calm her nerves before appearing on his Person to Person telecast.

Because of the continued legal wrangle over her contract with Twentieth Century-Fox, Marilyn was barred from being paid for performing or for public appearances. But Greene knew that it was vital to keep his partner in the public eye, so on March 31, the president of Marilyn Monroe Productions appeared before twenty-five thousand people in Madison Square Garden atop a pink-painted elephant named Karnaudi during a benefit for the Arthritis and Rheumatism Foundation. Marilyn's appearance—not to mention her extremely skimpy costume—was the big hit of the event, and the press wasted no time in giving her the publicity to which she had become accustomed in Hollywood. To handle the bombardment of requests for interviews and photographs of the rebellious star, Greene enlisted the aid of the Arthur Jacob's office of press representatives, which assigned agent Lois Weber. "In a matter of days I found myself protecting her just like the others were," Weber said.

Perhaps the biggest press coup of all occurred a week after her elephant ride.

Marilyn's 1955 move to New York brought her close to Arthur Miller, and the two began a romance that she had longed for since their first meeting. This photograph was taken a year before their marriage.

Edward R. Murrow, the famed journalist who hosted the popular interview show *Person to Person*, brought his television crew to the Greene home on Good Friday (April 8) for an informal visit with the Greenes and their famous guest. But Marilyn's extreme nervousness about talking live before millions of viewers, combined with a painful menstrual period that had to be numbed with pills, did little to help her dumb blonde image. Amy Greene was on hand to quickly fill in when Marilyn occasionally responded to Murrow's questions with confused silence. Amy was so adept in her task, in fact, that she won admirers nationwide.

Within days of Marilyn's television appearance, Greene decided that maintenance of her star status demanded more suitable environs than his rural farm, so he rented a luxurious suite for her at the Waldorf-Astoria Towers on Park Avenue at a rate of $1,000 a week. Greene footed the bill, as Marilyn was broke. He also bought Marilyn a black Thunderbird and assumed all her expenses, from beauty services and products to press agents, to care for her mother. Marilyn's psychiatric care would run up the tab further still—to about $50,000 by the end of 1955. (Apparently, Greene used all his resources, including his personal savings, credit, and the income from his studio to help support Marilyn.)

Despite her botched interview with Murrow, April brought a wealth of public attention and material comfort to Marilyn, and it marked the beginning of romance between her and playwright Arthur Miller, whom she hadn't seen since 1951. Even without the publicity surrounding her flight from Hollywood and New York activities, Miller could not have helped knowing Marilyn was in town because some of his closest friends—Eli Wallach and his wife, Anne Jackson, both of whom were Actors Studio devotees, and Norman Rosten, a college pal of Miller's from the University of Michigan—were also close to her. But Miller and Marilyn did not cross paths until April, when they were reunited at a theater-related party. They talked for a time, and after two weeks, Miller contacted Paula Strasberg to get Marilyn's phone number.

Miller, with his marriage on the verge of collapse, began seeing Marilyn discreetly at the homes of their mutual friends in Manhattan and Brooklyn Heights. When the couple did venture out together in public, whether on bike rides or for meals at obscure restaurants, they managed to go unrecognized. The press did not find out about the affair for almost a year, and even those in Marilyn's employ were unaware of the relationship.

DiMaggio and Marilyn remained on good terms despite their messy breakup. Here, he escorts her to the premiere of the movie that marked the end of their marriage.

If Joe DiMaggio knew about Marilyn's secret romance with Miller, he didn't let on publicly. Marilyn's ex-husband continued to hope for reconciliation, and even went to her journalist friends for advice on how to win her back. Marilyn refused to completely sever ties with DiMaggio, and they often went together to visit Fred Karger's sister, Mary, who had moved to New Jersey. On Marilyn's twenty-ninth birthday, June 1, 1955—the New York premiere of *The Seven Year Itch*, Marilyn's last movie as a "slave" to her studio—DiMaggio was by her side, despite his distaste for such events. He even threw a party in her honor at Toot Shor's, but Marilyn stormed out before the festivities could progress very far. She and DiMaggio had argued, and Marilyn left with Sam Shaw.

Another relationship that Marilyn had maintained over the years—but one lacking the volatile emotion of the DiMaggio tenure—was her friendship with Henry Rosenfeld. During the summer of 1955, the relationship apparently became romantic, and it has been said that Rosenfeld might even have proposed marriage. It is also rumored that Marilyn became involved that summer with Marlon Brando, an actor she fiercely admired and one who would remain her friend until her death, affair or no affair.

The summer of 1955 may have been a romantic time for Marilyn, but it was a difficult time for high-ranking executives at Twentieth Century-Fox, who were stewing over the fact that the star of their huge summer smash, *The Seven Year Itch*, was not committed to helping them make yet more money. The film was making millions of dollars, eliciting critical raves, and making Twentieth Century-Fox intensify negotiations to lure its hottest commodity back into its fold.

The hoopla surrounding the success of *The Seven Year Itch* had no apparent effect on Marilyn. Even the sight of the forty-foot-(12m)-high poster showing her skirt billowing high over her head moved her to comment simply, "That's the way they think of me." Marilyn seemed more interested in her pursuit of acting competence than in what was being said about her. Perhaps as part of her role as "the new Marilyn," she avoided publicity regarding her personal life, content to quietly pursue more rewarding experiences, such as going to Carnegie Hall, cooking for friends, and reading volumes of philosophical and classic literature. She enjoyed excursions to the country homes of the Greenes, Rostens, and Strasbergs. But in the midst of her personal and professional growth, there remained a haunting reliance on pills and alcohol to bring about the sleep that increasingly eluded her.

A workman erecting a giant cutout figure of Marilyn stops to take a look at those terrific legs in a reproduction of the famous scene from **The Seven Year Itch** *that he is installing in New York's Times Square.*

Marilyn Monroe Productions was one aspect of her life that Marilyn didn't have to worry about. Milton Greene was handling all the firm's business and bills, most of which involved Marilyn's personal care and expenses. He had mortgaged his personal properties and borrowed to raise

Sir Laurence Olivier joined Marilyn to announce Marilyn Monroe Productions' first project, The Prince and the Showgirl, but Marilyn's plunging neckline commanded much of the media attention.

funds while he continued working as a photographer for income. In addition to payments to keep Marilyn in a high-profile lifestyle, in early 1956 he invested in the firm's future by procuring the rights to Terence Rattigan's play *The Sleeping Prince*, which was developed into a film project within months as *The Prince and the Showgirl*. In the meantime, Greene found that Twentieth Century-Fox was taking a more conciliatory stance regarding Marilyn, and he was making progress toward a new contract for her.

Marilyn was also making progress. At the Actors Studio, Strasberg had been grooming her for her first stage appearance, and as 1955 drew to a close, he decided she was ready. At about the same time, Miller decided he was ready to make plans for a future with Marilyn, and by January 1956 columnist Earl Wilson had broken the story that Arthur and Mary Miller were getting divorced. With both her romance with Miller and her acting studies intensifying, Marilyn received word that a new contract was being worked out with Twentieth Century-Fox.

By late December Greene had negotiated new terms with the studio, which provided Marilyn a salary of $100,000 a year from Marilyn Monroe Productions beginning February 1, 1956, and allotted him $75,000 annu-

ally; paid Marilyn Monroe Productions $100,000 per film plus retroactive pay for Marilyn and a share of the profits, with almost 50 percent of that going to Greene; committed Marilyn to make a maximum of four films for Twentieth Century-Fox over the next seven years; and gave Marilyn director, cameraman, and concept approval for all her films. The official contract terms were announced January 4, 1956, and it was revealed that her first film for the studio would be *Bus Stop*, with approved director Joshua Logan, a former Stanislavsky student.

Marilyn was bound for a Hollywood homecoming in February to begin shooting *Bus Stop*, but before leaving New York she finally performed at the Actors Studio. She chose to portray the title character from Eugene O'Neill's *Anna Christie* and performed the opening scene with Maureen Stapleton. Despite trouble with remembering her lines in rehearsals, Marilyn was flawless during the scene, Stapleton recalled. Actress Kim Stanley said her performance was the first to elicit applause in the traditionally somber Actors Studio.

Another milestone for Marilyn took place on February 9, when she announced Marilyn Monroe Productions' first project, *The Prince and the Showgirl*. At her side for the Plaza Hotel press conference was her leading man and director, Sir Laurence Olivier. About two hundred press members covered the announcement—their critical reports reflected that most of them were uncomfortable with Marilyn's new role as producer and were somewhat perturbed in the knowledge that their coverage had helped her attain her new power. During the conference, the thin shoulder strap of Marilyn's dress snapped, and photographers swarmed the novice producer in pursuit of a clearer shot. Marilyn reportedly was angry at their apparent disregard for her distinguished costar, and the fact that they focused instead on her errant strap. Olivier later charged that she had planned the accident to get attention, but when one reporter there posed the question of whether the incident was planned, Marilyn stormed out of the conference.

Still denying that she and Miller planned to marry, Marilyn departed for Hollywood to play roadhouse singer Cherie in *Bus Stop*. Norman Rosten said of her departure: "Her success in facing a live audience [at the Actors Studio] infused Marilyn with a new confidence as she prepared a return to Hollywood.... And with it came audacious plans to break with the star system and take control of her destiny." But Marilyn left the East Coast with a promise to return, telling her wardrobe designer and friend, John Moore, "I'll be back when the picture is over. New York is my home now. Hollywood is just a place to work in." Hollywood also was a place to go to court in: Marilyn had left behind a 1954 outstanding warrant for driving without a license. She faced Judge Charles Griffin on February 28, and was fined $55.

When Marilyn arrived in Hollywood to start work on *Bus Stop*, a mob of fans and photographers welcomed her home. Her return coincided with a changing of the guard at Twentieth Century-Fox. Darryl Zanuck resigned less than a month later, and Maurice "Buddy" Adler, producer of *Bus Stop*, took the helm of the studio she had accused of

Above and opposite: **Bus Stop,** *Marilyn's first film after her split with Hollywood, benefited from her newly allowed creative input as well as her strengthened acting skills. Her performance as the showgirl Cherie is pointed to as probably her best.*

"screwing" her—"and I don't like to be screwed," she added—with her former contract salary. Strangely enough, Marilyn found that during her absence from the studio, her dressing room was undisturbed, except by the cleaning staff who dusted her sundry array of pill boxes, makeup supplies, unopened fan mail, and a framed photograph of DiMaggio.

Paula Strasberg, for whom Greene had arranged a salary from Twentieth Century-Fox as Marilyn's acting coach, accompanied Marilyn on her return. This effectively barred Natasha Lytess from playing any further role in Marilyn's career. Marilyn had not contacted Lytess since her move to New York; rather than personally inform her coach that her services no longer would be required, Marilyn had her attorneys contact Lytess, who was still employed by Fox, via telegram.

The Strasbergs' influence enveloped the *Bus Stop* set, and Logan feared Paula's presence would cause difficulty due to Marilyn's dependence on her, just as the star's relationship with Lytess had wreaked havoc on the sets of previous films. Logan attempted to bar Paula from the set, which prompted Lee Strasberg to contact him. Strasberg told the director of his immense respect for Marilyn's talents, saying that only Marlon Brando had shown as much potential. Logan relented somewhat regarding Paula, allowing her to be nearby for guidance "as long as it's clear to Paula she is never to come on the set."

For the first time, Marilyn had a say in how a film was to be made. One of her first contributions was to scrap the usual elaborate costume sketches in favor of personally searching through the wardrobe department for the most appropriate clothing she could find for her character. When she found the fishnet stockings that later would become so closely associated with the film, she ripped them and instructed wardrobe to make them look crudely darned. Greene contributed heavily to the film: he was hired to do the makeup and lighting, and gave the film a gritty, authentic look and feeling.

Logan was well aware of Marilyn's nervousness on past sets and was determined to be accommodating. He treated her as if she were fragile and managed to do so throughout numerous unusable takes as well as bouts of lateness on the part of his star, which she blamed on illness. His patience was almost limitless, but during location shooting in Phoenix, Arizona, for the rodeo and outdoor bus-stop scenes, he had to physically pull her from her dressing room and push her into a shot in which she runs down a street as the sun sets. Her health problems appeared to be genuine; one photographer said the only pictures he was able to get of Marilyn captured her getting sick under some bleachers between rodeo scenes. Upon her return to Hollywood in April for studio shooting, Marilyn was hospitalized for more than a week at Cedars of Lebanon Hospital, where she was diagnosed with acute bronchitis and exhaustion. In the interim, Logan filmed one of the longest fight shoots in history—fifteen days' worth of work for a half-minute clip.

As Logan labored to extract perhaps the finest performance Marilyn ever delivered, Arthur Miller wiled away his time with Saul Bellow at the Pyramid Lake Guest Ranch near Reno, Nevada, to obtain a divorce, just as Marilyn had done in Las Vegas ten years earlier. Perhaps Miller's situation added to Marilyn's anxiety while filming *Bus Stop*. Whatever the case, her New York psychiatrist eventually was flown in to help her through the rest of the film, and Logan finally was able to relax a bit. He arranged a cocktail party near the end of filming for President Achmed Sukarno of Indonesia, a fan of Marilyn's, who was being escorted in Hollywood by Logan's brother Marshall. Marilyn was invited at Sukarno's request, and he told her, "You are a very important person in Indonesia. Your pictures are the most popular of any that have ever played in my country. The entire Indonesian population is interested in meeting you." (A year later, after hearing news of an attempted coup against Sukarno, she suggested that she and Miller might offer him refuge in New York.)

Acute anxiety and health problems plagued Marilyn during the filming of Bus Stop, *but they didn't show on screen.*

When filming was over, despite all the problems, Logan had nothing but praise for Marilyn's work, calling her "the most completely realized and authentic actress since Garbo. Monroe is pure cinema. Watch her work…how rarely she has to use words. How much she does with her eyes, her lips, her slight, almost accidental gestures. She can become one of the greatest stars we've ever had—if she can control her emotions and her health." Biographer Fred Guiles wrote of her performance: "When Marilyn had recovered, and the film was nearing completion, it became evident that 'Bus Stop' was the most nearly perfect film of her career. She was as good as she would ever be, and that was very good indeed. She was more than worth all the fuss."

Shooting on *Bus Stop* was completed in May 1956, and two days after her thirtieth birthday, Marilyn returned to New York, carting with her a pregnant white Persian cat named Mitsou and a basset hound puppy called Hugo. Miller was still in Nevada, and while there he was subpoenaed to face the House Un-American Activities Committee (HUAC) in Washington, D.C. The group claimed it was investigating why Miller had been denied a passport two years earlier for suspected Communist "leanings"—an assessment Miller was fighting so he could accompany Marilyn to England later that year when shooting was to begin on *The Prince and the Showgirl*. Miller suspected the Committee was seizing a golden chance at publicity, having lost considerable steam since its "Red Scare" rise to prominence in 1947. What better publicity than that generated by the love interest of the nation's hottest movie star?

The subpoena aside, Miller's stay in Nevada had its advantages. As Marilyn revealed to a few confidantes, she and Miller solidified their intention to marry through numerous phone calls while he was there (she would call as "Mrs. Leslie," asking to speak with "Mr. Leslie"; these code names were inspired by characters who were involved in an affair in the Vina Delmar novel *About Mrs. Leslie*). Additionally, the desert's solitude enabled Miller to make progress on the play he was writing, and some of the area's colorful characters—namely, a group of renegade cowboys Miller met—inspired him to write a short story the next year called "The Misfits," which later evolved into a screenplay for Marilyn. Regarding his future plans with Marilyn, the only clue Miller gave was in a letter to his cousin Morton Miller, with whom he was especially close. Miller wrote: "When I return East, Morton, the shit will hit the fan."

Miller arrived in New York with his divorce papers about two weeks after Marilyn's return, and he immediately was surrounded by the press at the airport. At the Sutton Place apartment Greene had found for her, Marilyn awaited word that Miller had arrived. But the call was delayed for two hours, for Miller was bombarded with reporters' questions regarding possible marriage plans and his scheduled appearance before HUAC. Miller disclosed no personal plans. On June 20, Marilyn accompanied the playwright to

Not even pressure from the HUAC could put a damper on the romance between "the egghead and the hourglass" in mid-1956, since Miller had just attained his divorce decree and announced his intention to marry Marilyn before year's end.

Washington and waited for him the next day at the home of Miller's attorney, Joseph Raugh, where she faced the press and expressed her confidence that Miller "will win."

In the Caucus Room at the House building, Miller refused to name fellow attendees at Communist gatherings when he was involved in a Marxist study course almost two decades earlier, and he denied ever having been a member of the Communist Party. But he did reveal why he was fighting the State Department's denial of his passport request: "The objective is double. I have a production, which is in the talking stage in England, of 'A View From the Bridge,' and I will be there with the woman who will then be my wife."

Marilyn and Miller meet the press at his Connecticut farm on June 29, 1956, just hours before they dashed across the New York state line to be married in secret.

On the morning of the promised press conference, June 29, Miller called Marilyn's press agent, Lois Weber, seeking her help in handling the media and saying he was expecting "five or so reporters." She tried to explain to Miller that his farm would be overrun with reporters—"they'll be hanging from trees"—but even she was shocked at the huge number that actually came by. More than fifty reporters and photographers were counted on the back lawn—all of them a bit annoyed because the two people they had come to see were nowhere to be found.

At around 1:15 P.M., above the loud buzz of the press crowd, a crashing sound was heard. Minutes later, Miller and Marilyn drove up with Miller's cousin Morton, who was driving the car. Unknown to the press, the three had been across the New York state line to obtain a marriage license. Miller dashed for the house, leaving a dazed-looking Marilyn seated in the car. After a few minutes, an obviously shaken Morton informed the press that a car following theirs had crashed into a tree, throwing *Paris-Match*'s New York bureau chief, Mara Sherbatoff, through the windshield. The woman lay bleeding just a short distance up the road, and she died later that afternoon of her injuries. Miller had run into the house to summon help, and Marilyn, seemingly on the verge of hysteria and too shaky to walk on her own, was helped to the house.

Once inside, Marilyn regained her composure enough to censure Lois Weber for allowing television crews to set up sound equipment outside. The photographers were pacified when Marilyn came out and posed for pictures; Miller and his parents then joined her for a family portrait. Miller managed to avoid giving the gathered reporters any concrete information, such as when he and Marilyn planned to be married. In the house, however, Miller made his intentions very clear: he wanted to be wed that evening.

Calls were made to lawyers, local authorities, and close friends, including the Strasbergs. They all were to converge outside the courthouse in White Plains, New York, just across the Connecticut state line. Judge Seymour Rabinowitz delayed his own anniversary plans to perform the civil ceremony, and Miller borrowed his mother's wedding band to place on the bride's finger.

This revelation set off a flurry of activity; Marilyn's Sutton Place apartment was surrounded by reporters, so when the couple returned to New York, they immediately left with Miller's parents, Isidore and Augusta, in search of some peace at Miller's Roxbury, Connecticut, farm. Miller staved off the hordes of reporters from the farm with the promise of a press conference at the end of the week, and the couple enjoyed relative peace while working out their wedding plans. Marilyn sought instruction from Augusta in preparing authentic Jewish foods and, determined to adopt the faith of her husband-to-be and most of her New York friends, received instruction in Judaism from Rabbi Robert Goldburg, who agreed to perform the wedding ceremony on July 1.

Wearing a wedding gown for the second and last time in her life, Marilyn dresses in sheath champagne and chiffon for a Jewish wedding ceremony with Arthur Miller on July 1. In Miller's parents, Isidore and Augusta, Marilyn found the family she had always longed for.

Two days later, again unknown to the press, Miller and Marilyn had the Jewish ceremony they had originally planned at the home of Miller's literary agent, Kay Brown. There were about thirty guests, and Marilyn wore a bone-white gown and veil dyed with tea leaves to match. Later that week Miller presented her with a gold band inscribed "A. to M., June 1956. Now is Forever."

The couple received a wedding present of sorts from the State Department: Miller's passport. Apparently the department had been shamed into approving Miller's passport application by the foreign press, who were highly critical of America's treatment of one of its most important playwrights. But Miller also received news that Congress threatened to cite him for contempt if he didn't start "naming names" by a certain deadline—meaning a possible fine of up to $1,000 and one year in jail if found guilty. Miller's reaction was to plan the trip to England with his famous bride.

Two weeks after they were married, Marilyn and Miller made their way through a throng of reporters as they boarded their plane for England (Miller described the walk to the plane as a little like drowning). They were met at the London airport on July 14 by Sir Laurence Olivier and his wife, actress Vivien Leigh, who had played Marilyn's role of showgirl Elsie Marina opposite Olivier in the successful English stage version of *The Sleeping Prince.* Alongside the Millers were Hedda Rosten, on hand as Marilyn's secretary-companion; the Greenes; and Paula Strasberg. The English press focused immediately on Marilyn, but they soon turned against her when she uncharacteristically passed on numerous publicity opportunities; they labeled her a pretentious snob.

The Millers found solitude at a rented country mansion in Egham while Olivier fretted about how to handle Marilyn. Logan, his experiences during *Bus Stop* fresh in his mind, advised, "Load up the camera and put

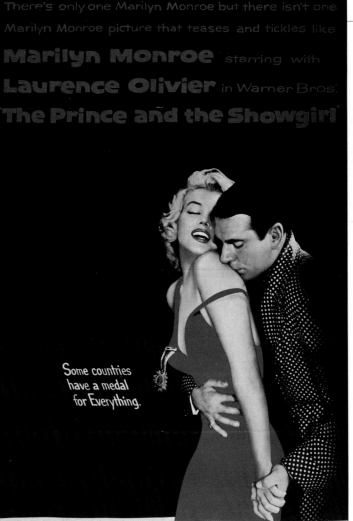

There's only one Marilyn Monroe but there isn't one Marilyn Monroe picture that teases and tickles like

Marilyn Monroe starring with **Laurence Olivier** in Warner Bros. **"The Prince and the Showgirl"**

Some countries have a medal for Everything.

Marilyn in front of it, and keep Paula Strasberg, whom I love dearly and who seems to be giving Marilyn something she needs, away from the set." And Logan repeatedly stressed, "Don't order [Marilyn] about, because it'll throw her and you won't get anything out of her."

Olivier, perhaps determined that Marilyn portray Elsie Marina as Leigh had, quickly lost his patience with her. In desperation, he turned to Paula Strasberg for assistance, allowing her on the Pinewood Studios set despite Logan's repeated warnings. In doing so, he further alienated himself from his costar, who would turn to Paula to supplement Olivier's direction.

Relations between Olivier and Marilyn deteriorated further when she resumed her pattern of tardiness and outright absenteeism, missing entire days of shooting rather than face Olivier. Miller bore the burden of getting Marilyn to the set—a role she resented him playing—and he sometimes managed to get her there four or more hours late. But few could fathom the huge obstacles Miller faced in this task: Marilyn's problems with insomnia often kept her awake until the morning hours, and as the night progressed she would get hysterical about not being able to sleep.

To compound her existing anxiety, about six weeks into shooting, Marilyn claimed to find some critical notes that her new husband had written about her. She told the Strasbergs, "It was something about how disappointed he was in me. How he thought I was some kind of angel but now he guessed he was wrong. That his first wife had let him down, but I had done something worse. Olivier was beginning to think I was a troublesome bitch and that he, Arthur, no longer had a decent answer to that one." (Marilyn would never forgive Miller for his "betrayal"; she would remind him of it at stressful times in their marriage.)

To make things worse, Marilyn's relationship with Greene was also under strain. Marilyn was becoming cool toward her business partner possibly due to Miller's growing influence and the fact that he was never happy with Greene's role in managing Marilyn's business affairs. Another factor could have been Greene's hiring of Olivier as director for *The Prince and the Showgirl* without what Marilyn perceived to be concrete approval from Lee Strasberg.

In England the rift between Marilyn and Greene widened when Greene discussed plans with *Prince* cinematographer Jack Cardiff to establish an English subsidiary of Marilyn Monroe Productions in order to make British films with Cardiff as director. The Millers were surprised and angered to read about these plans in newspaper reports. (The plans were dropped; Cardiff went on to become a very successful director.) The Millers offered Greene $500,000 for his shares of Marilyn Monroe Productions, but he refused.

Apparently, Marilyn's pill use was at frightening levels during filming. Besides the barbiturates she took at night for her insomnia, under Miller's watchful eye, Greene said he supplied amphetamines for her in the morning, and Paula made sure they were always available to Marilyn on the set. Again, her New York therapist was flown in to help her function. The doctor's arrival gave Olivier the opportunity to dismiss Paula, by now suffering from jangled nerves as well, and she returned to New York. Marilyn began showing up regularly for work, especially after Olivier boosted her confidence by passing on an inspiring observation by Dame Sybil Thorndike, who said: "We need her desperately. She's the only one of us who really knows how to act in front of a camera."

On November 17, production was complete and, thanks to Greene's monumental efforts behind the scenes as go-between and fence-mender, within budget. Just before filming concluded, Marilyn was invited to appear at a Royal

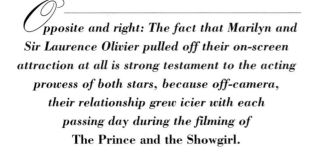

Opposite and right: The fact that Marilyn and Sir Laurence Olivier pulled off their on-screen attraction at all is strong testament to the acting prowess of both stars, because off-camera, their relationship grew icier with each passing day during the filming of **The Prince and the Showgirl.**

On October 29, 1956, Marilyn was presented to Queen Elizabeth at the Empire Theatre in London's Leicester Square.

Command Film Performance for a screening of *The Battle of the River Plate*. She was presented to Queen Elizabeth and managed a proper curtsy, which she told the queen she had to master for scenes in *The Prince and the Showgirl*. Perhaps mustering up even more courage than when meeting the queen, Marilyn faced the *Prince* crew before her departure and announced, "I hope you will all forgive me, as it wasn't altogether my fault. I have been ill." But through it all, Marilyn mustered enough magic to make Olivier write of the finished picture in his memoirs: "I was as good as could be, and Marilyn! Marilyn was quite wonderful, the best of all. What do you know?"

On January 3, 1957, the Millers finally took their long-delayed honeymoon. Accompanied by Morton Miller and his wife, Marilyn and Arthur stayed at a villa overlooking the sea in Ocho Rios, Jamaica, until January 19. Once they returned to New York City, Marilyn and Miller settled into a thirteenth-floor apartment with a view of the East River at 444 East Fifty-seventh Street. Marilyn resumed her Actors Studio classes with the Strasbergs, and Miller labored over his typewriter in the study Marilyn had reserved for him in the apartment. (Miller had sold his Roxbury farm while in England.)

Taking an extended break from her film career, Marilyn threw herself into the role of wife and stepmother to Miller's children, Robert and Jane, and found a degree of peace. She hosted parties for her closest friends and accompanied Miller on biking and boating excursions in Central Park. But with their newfound contentment came unwanted headlines: Miller was found guilty in contempt-of-Congress proceedings, and the "Wrong Door Raid" inquiries had begun. Like DiMaggio, Marilyn avoided testifying about the 1954 incident since she was no longer in California. Also, Marilyn's involvement with Slatzer during her 1952 DiMaggio courtship was revealed in a tabloid, although their unrecorded marriage remained a secret.

While domestic bliss was bringing Miller and Marilyn closer, Marilyn's partnership with Greene continued to deteriorate. In the spring of 1957, Greene finally sold his share of the company's stock for no more than $100,000. "My interest in Marilyn's career was not for gain," he said when explaining the buyout. "She needed me at the time, and I put at her complete disposal whatever abilities I possessed." The board of directors had lost a vice president, but Miller's brother-in-law and one of his friends took Greene's place.

Twelve days after Marilyn's thirty-first birthday, Marilyn and Miller attended the premiere of *The Prince and the Showgirl* at Radio City Music Hall. While some reviewers declared Marilyn's Elsie "a dumb, affable showgirl and nothing more," others touted Marilyn's performance as "triumphant," "sparkling," and "a most pleasant surprise." To distance themselves from the critics and to escape the stifling heat in New York City, the Millers decided to rent a private beach cottage at Amagansett on Long Island.

Shortly after arriving at Amagansett, Marilyn found out she was pregnant, and the couple was overjoyed. Miller wrote in the mornings, successfully penning his short story "The Misfits," while Marilyn tended the garden; in the afternoon they often enjoyed surf fishing. But their happiness ended abruptly one day in August when, responding to Marilyn's screams, Miller found her doubled over in pain during her sixth week of pregnancy. She was rushed to New York's Doctors Hospital, where her physician found the pregnancy to be tubal and had the embryo, which was developing outside the womb, removed.

On the surface, Marilyn seemed to recover quickly, going so far as to reschedule a party that had been postponed by the emergency. But privately, she was becoming despondent. She increasingly turned to pills for relief, and she had numerous "false" pregnancies. Her friend Henry Rosenfeld recalled: "She wanted a baby so much that she'd convince herself [she was pregnant] every two or three months. She'd gain maybe fourteen or fifteen pounds [6 or 7kg]." To cheer Marilyn, Miller promised to write a movie based on his short story "The Misfits" for her. This prospect helped her mood for a few days, but one afternoon Miller saw his wife fall into a chair and start dozing immediately; soon her breathing became labored. Realizing she had overdosed on pills, Miller called for medical assistance. Sadly, many similar scenes were repeated throughout their marriage.

At the end of the summer, the Millers returned to their New York apartment, much to the delight of Marilyn's devoted fans. Miller knew that the bustling city would infuse new energy into his wife. Although she was not actively involved in the film industry, offers were pouring in. In one instance earlier in the year, Greene had turned down a $2 million offer for a Marilyn Monroe television series because she wasn't "up to the strain." Without Greene to manage these and other business affairs in New York, Marilyn hired May Reis, formerly an employee of Elia Kazan, to handle the influx of offers and correspondence.

Miller found it difficult to concentrate on writing in the New York apartment, so when the 110-acre (40ha) Leavenworth homestead adjacent to his previous Roxbury home was put on the market in late 1957, he and Marilyn bought it. The couple divided their time between the city and the farm, putting much of their energies into renovation of the two-story, eighteenth-century farmhouse, against the advice of everyone who had seen the dilapidated building—including noted architect Frank Lloyd Wright, whom Marilyn consulted. The renovation was a seemingly never-ending project, although Marilyn and Arthur did successfully add a new wing they called the nursery and built a private cabin that Miller would use as a writing workshop.

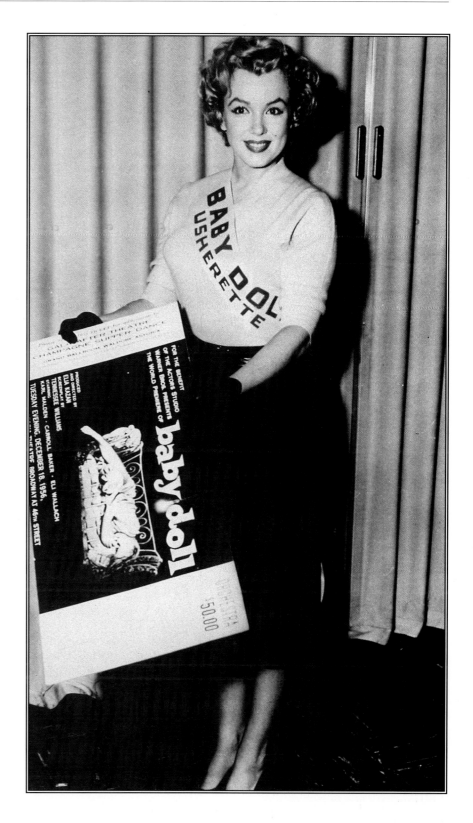

Marilyn was very charitable, as evidenced by her 1956 stint as a movie usherette.

Time spent at the Connecticut farm, just extended weekends at first, were very productive for Miller. Besides progress on the old house, thanks to the efforts of an ever-present carpenter, Miller was penning a new story, "Please Don't Kill Anything," that would provide the impetus for Marilyn's character in the film version of "The Misfits."

"Please Don't Kill Anything" was a story inspired by Marilyn's heartbreak over seeing harm come to any animal. Even in Jamaica she had thrown beached fish, although obviously dead, back into the sea as if that would bring them back to life. She would become hysterical at the sight of a suffering animal and cry easily over a flower being cut before its natural demise. She surrounded herself with pets—her hound, Hugo; a horse, bought for the farm, that she rarely rode; and a couple of talking parakeets. When her cat, Mitsou, had its kittens, Marilyn helped deliver the litter and called more than a half dozen vets for advice on proper care. If only she could have shown herself as much compassion.

For almost two years, Miller and Marilyn stayed out of the public spotlight. Marilyn continued studying at the Actors Studio and held a reunion cookout-swim for her most devoted fans, the Monroe Six and James Haspiel, at the Connecticut farm. But for all the contentment her life now offered, she drank heavily, continued her destructive pill taking, and had to be "saved" by Miller time and again. One evening in 1958 at a party, Norman Rosten, sensing Marilyn was again slipping into a morose mood, had her agree to a pact that if either of them ever entertained suicidal thoughts, the other would be called as a safety net. She agreed and would agree to similar pacts with other friends in coming months.

Aside from a few short stories, Miller's career languished during his first two years of marriage to Marilyn, but he did manage to turn out the first draft of the screenplay for The Misfits. He showed the screenplay to his friend and former editor, Frank Taylor, who spent a lot of time, along with his wife, Nan, with Miller and Marilyn. Taylor was so excited over the screenplay that he sent it to John Huston, who was in Paris working on a film; Huston wired back that the work was magnificent and that he wanted to be a part of it. A copy also was sent to Clark Gable, Miller's first choice for the lead, and Gable responded by asking when production could begin.

Before Marilyn could work on The Misfits, however, she had to do a film for United Artists called Some Like It Hot, followed by one for Twentieth Century-Fox to help fulfill her contractual obligation.

Marilyn returned to Hollywood in July 1958, and the press jammed the airport. In her usual fashion, although the plane was on time, she managed to be late, getting off the plane thirty minutes after all the other passengers. "I'm sorry," she cooed to reporters. "I was asleep." When production of Some Like It Hot began on August 4, Marilyn was accompanied to the soundstage by a large entourage— Miller, coach Paula Strasberg, a hairdresser, a makeup man, and a press agent, among others. Director Billy Wilder, still wincing from his experiences with Marilyn on The Seven Year Itch, found out from the start that getting through to his very fragile star for this picture would be a monumental effort.

Again, whether purposefully or not, Marilyn angered the cast and crew by arriving hours late for a scheduled shoot (although Miller assured Wilder that Marilyn left each morning for the studio by 7 A.M.). It was no secret that she resented playing second fiddle to the antics of her costars, Tony Curtis and Jack Lemmon. (Lemmon took the role Marilyn hoped her close friend Frank Sinatra [Sinatra and Marilyn remained friends despite the "Wrong Door Raid"] would portray, but Sinatra failed to show up for a meeting with Wilder, much to Marilyn's dismay.) She also had fought the decision to shoot the film in black and white, and she wasn't happy about resuming her "dumb blonde" characterization, either. She infuriated Wilder by

To the English press while shooting *The Prince and the Showgirl*:

Q.:

What inspired you to study acting?

M.:

Seeing my own pictures.

reportedly telling his assistant director, sent to pry Marilyn from her dressing room, to "go f---" himself. Lemmon and Curtis tired of her tardiness before they might have under different circumstances, perhaps because their wait consisted of standing around in high heels, dresses, stuffed bras, and layers of pasty makeup for their portrayal of two musicians posing as members of an all-girl band in order to escape a murderous mob. Both characters had set their amorous sights on a sweet, blonde, bourbon-sneaking ukulele player named Sugar Kane, portrayed by Marilyn.

When Marilyn finally did show up on the set, she had difficulty delivering even the simplest dialogue; one scene in which she had a single line—"It's me, Sugar"—required forty-seven takes. In another scene, where she rummages through a drawer and asks, "Where's that bourbon?" required so many takes that Wilder finally taped the words inside the drawer so she could get it right. Unfortunately, Curtis and Lemmon suffered through the dozens of takes, losing the spark of their original delivery as Marilyn gradually improved. Utterly exasperated, Curtis blurted out while watching the rushes that his love scenes with Marilyn were about as romantic for him as "kissing Hitler."

In Marilyn's defense, her distraction during filming probably was compounded by the fact that she had recently found out she was pregnant. But her mood and memory for dialogue improved temporarily in September when the cast hit Coronado Beach, just north of the Mexico border, for a week of location shots. She told Miller the beach would "be great for the baby." But upon her return to Hollywood, she was admitted to the hospital briefly, suffering from "nervous exhaustion." As on her last two films, Marilyn's psychotherapist was flown in from New York, this time joined by her medical doctor.

The stories surrounding the disasters during the making of *Some Like It Hot* have become ingrained in Hollywood lore. But no one will deny that Marilyn's insistence upon reshooting her introductory scene in the movie—which originally consisted of a simple zoom-in as she played the ukulele—added a distinctive spark as it instead treated moviegoers to a memorable view of her trademark wiggle. And just as terrific as the fine-tuned romantic comedy were her musical numbers. When filming ended on November 6, *Some Like It Hot* was several hundred thousand dollars over budget, costing about $2.8 million. But moviegoers found it worth

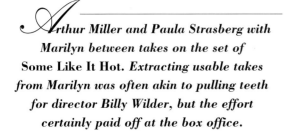

Arthur Miller and Paula Strasberg with Marilyn between takes on the set of Some Like It Hot. Extracting usable takes from Marilyn was often akin to pulling teeth for director Billy Wilder, but the effort certainly paid off at the box office.

Tony Curtis on Memories of Marilyn

Tony Curtis' work with Marilyn Monroe has been overshadowed by his off-the-cuff remark that the love scenes they shared in Some Like It Hot, *Marilyn's most successful film, were about as romantic as "kissing Hitler." But in late May 1991, just days before what would have been her sixty-fifth birthday, he offered a different point of view during a tribute to his late costar. Curtis offered the following remarks as a special speaker at the Polaroid "OneFilm Legendary Look-Alike Contest" held at Mann's Chinese Theater:*

"Marilyn was an interesting woman, a woman that I found intriguing and very complex. You could like her a great deal and you could dislike her at the same time. She was very personable and could be very alienating as well at the same time. I always liked Marilyn because she was true to what she represented, which was just being what she was—a woman....It wasn't easy for her in those early days in Hollywood. It wasn't easy for any of us. It was a big struggle to try to make something of ourselves.

"I am interested really, and intrigued, by all of the attention paid to this woman who's now dead a number of years. What was that element that keeps her alive in our memories and minds? I think I've got a theory: Marilyn represents to us in this country, and to the whole world, the possibility of becoming successful, rich, famous, happy—all of

Behind-the-scenes tension on Some Like It Hot spawned a lot of movie lore, but Tony Curtis remembers his costar "with great affection."

the elements that each one of us would like to represent or have—by just our looks. We talk of acting talent. I feel that there are no bad actors, just bad parts. That all of us can fit a role in life and all of us can play parts.

"Marilyn was the most beautiful woman that I've ever remembered seeing—magnificent-looking woman. Yet behind those pale eyes of hers was someone who was tortured and unhappy. I didn't find that unique, because I can look at anybody and find a little torture and pain. So she was very human. Her beauty is what catapulted her up on the screen, and her knowledge of herself. She was a gifted actress. She had a way of pretending and playing who she was.

"Yes, I do remember Marilyn with great affection."

every cent and then some: when *Some Like It Hot* premiered the next year it became the highest-grossing comedy film Hollywood had ever known.

Wilder threw a party to celebrate the film's completion, but he didn't invite Marilyn. Being left off the party guest list was the least of her concerns. Her pregnancy was her top priority, and after filming she returned to the hospital, then took to her bed at the Bel-Air Hotel before returning to New York (she rode to the airport in an ambulance as a precautionary measure). A few weeks later, on December 17, 1958, near the end of her first trimester of pregnancy, Marilyn lost her baby.

While the fragile star lapsed again into depression over her loss (which Miller blamed to a degree on the physical exertion demanded of her for a few *Some Like It Hot* scenes), her fans had their spirits lifted by a series of photographs featured in the December 22 issue of *Life* magazine. Photographer Richard Avedon had shot a spectacular series featuring Marilyn's interpretations of Theda Bara, Clara Bow, Marlene Dietrich, Lillian Russell, and her longtime idol, Jean Harlow. (Marilyn recently had passed up the opportunity to play Harlow; after looking at the script she said, "I hope they don't do that to me after I'm gone.")

After that, the next time the public saw Marilyn was at the Broadway premiere of *Some Like It Hot* on March 29, 1959, at Loew's Capitol Theatre. But her appearance was shaky: she lacked her usual public confidence and even reverted at times to her childhood stammer. Two months later she flew to Italy to accept the David di Donatello Award—the Italian equivalent of the Oscar—for her performance in *The Prince and the Showgirl*. The prize gave her a much-needed boost of confidence.

When Marilyn returned to America, she underwent corrective surgery to increase her chances for bearing children. But as her efforts to have a child intensified, her relationship with Miller seemed to be on a downward spiral. Even before her pregnancy during *Some Like It Hot*, Marilyn confided to Rosten, "Arthur says he wants [to have a child], but he's losing his enthusiasm."

Everyone close to the Millers sensed the growing tension between them. Marilyn would give her husband demeaning tasks, such as making

Miller wrote "The Misfits" for Marilyn in an attempt to bring back his wife's smile after her miscarriage.

him hold her purse for her, sending him on meaningless errands, and generally treating him more like a servant than a husband. His reaction was to comply without emotion, but he began to withdraw from his wife. Against this backdrop of gradual disintegration, Marilyn flew to the West Coast in September 1959 to attend a party for Soviet premier Nikita Khrushchev. Miller decided not to attend due to his troubles before the HUAC, despite his acquittal of contempt charges the previous year.

Twentieth Century-Fox was hosting a luncheon for the premier, and Marilyn, who had taken an increased interest in politics, was excited at the chance to help thaw the Cold War. Her escort in Miller's stead was his close friend Frank Taylor, whom Marilyn had chosen to produce *The Misfits*, due to begin production the next summer. Shortly after daybreak on the morning of the luncheon, Marilyn started getting ready; she spent more than two hours on her beauty preparations. To the delight of studio head Spyros Skouras, who had shown up at her Beverly Hills Hotel bungalow to make sure she would be there, Marilyn was actually early for the noon luncheon.

When Marilyn was introduced to Khrushchev, the premier took her hand and told her, "You're a very lovely young lady." Marilyn never discussed their conversation, but she was overheard to have replied, "My husband, Arthur Miller, sends you his greetings. There should be more of this kind of thing. It would help both our countries understand each other." Afterward, she told her maid Lena Pepitone, "I could tell Khrushchev liked me. He smiled more when he was introduced to me than for anyone else at the whole banquet. [Other guests included Elizabeth Taylor and Debbie Reynolds.] He squeezed my hand so long and hard I thought he would break it. I guess it was better than having to kiss him, though."

Back in New York that September, the Millers and Rostens attended a one-man Broadway show featuring Yves Montand. Miller admired the actor, who had starred in the French adaptation of *The Crucible*, one of Miller's last successes. Miller also could relate to Montand's trouble in gaining entry to the United States (the actor had been denied a visa until 1959 because he refused to answer on the application whether he was a Communist). Another prominent audience member was also impressed by Montand: George Cukor, who was to direct Marilyn's upcoming film, *Let's Make Love*.

Because Cukor admired Montand's Broadway performance, he suggested the Frenchman for the lead role in the film when Twentieth Century-Fox was having trouble finding an actor to play the part. Gregory Peck had agreed to portray the lead, but he walked off the production after Miller revised the script to better focus on Marilyn's role. After the lead was refused by Yul Brynner, Cary Grant, Charlton Heston, and Rock Hudson, Montand was given the part. Still, the part was a coup for Montand, for although he was a major star in Europe, he still was looking for his first American film role.

A romance with Yves Montand on the set of **Let's Make Love** *temporarily boosted Marilyn's spirits.*

Marilyn returned to Hollywood to begin filming *Let's Make Love* in February 1960. She and Miller stayed in a bungalow at the Beverly Hills Hotel, right across the hallway from Montand and his wife, actress Simone Signoret. Marilyn and Simone struck up a friendship immediately; they spent a great deal of time shopping, cooking, and talking together, and Montand was often the topic of conversation. When Marilyn heard about the actor's struggles—the poverty of his family during his youth, his lack of a formal education (he was a dropout), his reliance on his sex appeal to make headway in his career, and his quest for artistic recognition—she developed a feeling of empathy with and a deep

Yves Montand attained his first American film role with some help from Arthur Miller, whom he repaid by having an affair with Marilyn.

admiration for the actor. But that didn't spare Montand from Marilyn's usual bad habits. As with all of her costars of recent years, she kept the actor waiting on the set.

One day after Marilyn didn't show up on the set (Miller was in Europe to confer with John Huston on *Misfits* business), Montand and Signoret slid a note under Marilyn's door. The note read: "Next time you decide to hang around too late listening to my wife tell you stories instead of going to bed, because you've already decided not to get up the next morning and go to the studio, please tell me. I'm not the enemy. I'm your pal. And capricious little girls have never amused me." Perhaps the note struck a chord—Marilyn became much more punctual. Another event that may have made her more agreeable was the Golden Globe Awards, which honored her with the Best Actress in a Comedy or Musical award for her work in *Some Like It Hot*.

About six weeks into the shooting of *Let's Make Love*, an actors' strike was called, and all production ceased. Miller saw the strike as an opportunity to go to Nevada to scout *Misfit* locations. Around this time, Signoret was informed she would have to fly to Europe within ten days to begin work on a film. Montand started complaining to friends that Marilyn, left alone in the neighboring bungalow, was beginning to "throw herself" at him, but privately he didn't seem to mind her attentions. Author Fred Guiles wrote of the ensuing and hardly secretive affair: "[Marilyn] felt she had been set adrift by Miller, and that only a close emotional attachment could keep her from floundering," although the writer also observed that by the time filming began on *Let's Make Love*, Miller's role had been reduced from husband, lover, and friend to "a guardian who slept with her and counted her pills."

The Montand-Marilyn affair quickly became known in Hollywood circles. But Montand was not the only thing on Marilyn's mind during the spring of 1960. She had become increasingly involved in political affairs; among these, reportedly, was Senator John F. Kennedy's presidential campaign. As a registered Democrat in Connecticut, Marilyn was named an alternative delegate in April by the town of Roxbury for the presidential primaries, and attended fund-raising and other functions involving the senator at the beach home of Peter Lawford. (Marilyn had met Lawford in 1951 and reluctantly dated him, yet they remained on friendly terms. Lawford had since married Senator Kennedy's sister, Patricia.) Marilyn joined Lawford and a few other stars as sponsors of SANE, the National Committee for a Sane Nuclear Policy.

When filming of *Let's Make Love* was completed that summer, shortly after Marilyn's thirty-fourth birthday, Montand was heading back to Paris to join his wife. Marilyn had returned to New York before his departure and intercepted him at the airport, where his plane had a layover before crossing the Atlantic. Marilyn and Montand were seen talking and drinking champagne in the back of her limousine, but besides delaying his reunion with his wife by a few hours, Marilyn's efforts to keep him in New York (she had even reserved a hotel room) had no effect. He was intent on ending the affair.

A more enduring relationship for Marilyn that began during *Let's Make Love* was with Dr. Ralph Greenson, a psychiatrist who had been asked to counsel her by her New York doctor, Dr. Marianne Kris. Greenson's initial consultations with Marilyn revealed a fragile, deeply disturbed woman who was bordering on schizophrenia. He deviated from his usual Freudian therapies to provide more immediate help, and his first attempts centered on reducing her reliance on drugs. He was alarmed to learn over time how severely she abused drugs, sometimes taking them intravenously to speed their effect, and how she would go from doctor to doctor to obtain more drugs. He tried, with little success, to reteach her how to sleep without barbiturates. The doctor wrote: "I told her that she already received so much medication that it would put five other people to sleep, but the reason she wasn't sleeping was because she was afraid of sleeping. I promised she would sleep with less medication if she would recognize she is fighting sleep as well as searching for some oblivion which is not sleep." Greenson would continue to help the dependent patient until her death.

Still sporting their wedding bands, Marilyn and Montand attended some parties as a couple during the filming of Let's Make Love.

Chapter Five

"Misfit" to the End

When I was a kid, the world often seemed

a pretty grim place. I loved to escape through games

and make-believe. You can do that even better

as an actress, but sometimes it seems

you escape altogether and people

never let you come back. You're trapped

in your fame. Maybe I'll never

get out of it now until it's over.

On July 20, 1960, just days after *Let's Make Love* was complete, Marilyn flew with Miller to Reno, Nevada, to begin production of *The Misfits* with her idol, Clark Gable; her friend Eli Wallach; and Montgomery Clift, whom she also idolized, but with whom she had become good friends after their meeting two years earlier. (She then referred to Clift as "the only person I know who's in worse shape than I am.")

Arthur Miller had devoted his creative energies to the film's screenplay since the summer of 1957. Although the screenplay began as a testament of love, a gift to ease his wife's grief over the loss of her unborn child, *The Misfits* would turn out to be Miller's final contribution to Marilyn's personal and professional life.

Marilyn's troubled personality and her intense regard for animals were at the core of the film, in which she would portray Roslyn, an Easterner who had come to Reno for a divorce. Roslyn meets and falls for a rugged cowboy (played by Gable) who teams up with the characters played by Wallach and Clift to hunt wild horses, which they intend to sell to be slaughtered and used for dog food. Roslyn forces the men to reevaluate their intention, as she wants the horses spared. The film was to be shot in black and white and, unlike most movies, would be shot in sequence.

When the cast and crew (including Paula Strasberg) arrived in the Nevada desert, temperatures were already above 100ºF (37.8ºC). The only coolness on the set was Marilyn's treatment of Miller. For appearances' sake, they shared a suite at the Mapes Hotel and sometimes sat together at lunch. In addition to the grudges Marilyn bore, she also was less than pleased with Miller's screenplay (even though he continued making revisions until filming was complete, and even had to borrow the crew's generator one evening when nearby fires caused a power failure and prevented him from working after dark). "He could have written me anything, and he comes up with this," Marilyn said toward the end of filming. "If that's what he thinks of me, well, then, I'm not for him and he's not for me." The movie was "really about the cowboys and the horses," she said. "They don't need me at all; not to act—just for the money, to put my name on the marquee."

Since she was far away from her new psychiatrist, Dr. Greenson, and was unable to summon his help, Marilyn increased her

Part of the cast and crew of **The Misfits** *put their best face forward for a 1960 family portrait in the stifling Nevada heat.*

intake of pills. Director John Huston estimated that while working she took up to twenty pills a day, and washed them down with alcohol. Without the presence of someone like Montand to get her to the set on time (Montand had boasted during the filming of *Let's Make Love* that "she'll do whatever I ask her to do," including showing up on schedule), Marilyn reverted to her tardy ways on the day of her very first scene.

The first call for the scene, in which she had only three lines, was for 10 A.M.; at 11 A.M., Marilyn had yet to arrive. Biographer Fred Guiles wrote: "From that morning on, the truth began to seep through the company that Marilyn was terribly ill with insomnia and emotional problems. Her intake of Nembutal had risen from three or four a night to what would be a lethal dose for the average person. She required the attentions of several persons to get her in walking condition in the morning."

On July 30 and August 1, the tenth and eleventh days of production, Marilyn failed to show up for work, saying she was "indisposed." She managed to make it to the set the next few weeks, and enjoyed an August outing to Lake Tahoe's Cal-Neva Lodge with the entire *Misfits* company to see her old friend Frank Sinatra perform (Sinatra was in the process of buying the casino-resort). But on August 27, Huston halted shooting. Marilyn had been driven to the set and helped from the car to her camera spot, but when cameraman Russell Metty closed in on Marilyn for the camera shot, he told Huston her eyes wouldn't focus and that nothing could be done with her that day. Huston stopped production, and Marilyn—wrapped in a wet sheet to protect her from the heat—was flown back to Los Angeles for treatment under Dr. Greenson and physician Hyman Engelberg. Press agent Rupert Allan announced that she was suffering from exhaustion.

For the next ten days at Westside Hospital, Marilyn was gradually withdrawn from Nembutal and given a milder drug to help her sleep. Dr. Greenson found out she had made the rounds of doctors in Reno to procure her supply of Nembutal on location. Miller visited her once during her hospital stay, as did DiMaggio. But Marilyn had hoped for solace from another man, Montand, who had returned to America from Europe. She tried repeatedly to phone him, but he refused to take or return her calls.

Energized from her rest and doctors' care, Marilyn was bound for Nevada on September 5, and stopped in San Francisco on the way to see DiMaggio. Shooting resumed the next day, but a week later—and on at least two other occasions—production was halted again due to Marilyn's absence. However, *The Misfits* almost made the revised completion deadline of October 15. On October 17, the crew invited Marilyn to a surprise birthday party for Clift and Miller, and she surprised them by accepting. (This was the last social event Marilyn and Miller attended as husband and wife.)

Starring opposite Clark Gable was a dream come true for Marilyn, but was not enough to keep her punctual—or stable—during filming.

After the dinner party, the guests went to the adjoining casino to shoot craps. When Marilyn was handed the dice, she said to Huston, "What should I ask the dice for, John?" He answered, "Don't think honey, just throw. That's the story of your life. Don't think, do it." The roll turned out to be a lucky one, and location shooting was completed the next day.

When the crew reassembled in Hollywood at the Paramount lot that United Artists had borrowed for filming, the schedule was changed to one more favorable to Marilyn's habits—a union-approved 12-to-6 P.M. workday. Before the final shots were filmed, United Artists production chief Max Youngstein viewed the footage and told producer Frank Taylor he was disappointed in the film's progress, that he wanted to see more conflict among the main characters. So with input from Huston and Taylor, Miller—who by now had moved out of his wife's hotel suite—began rewriting the weaker scenes. This process was halted when Gable, the only cast member with script approval, flatly refused to shoot any revisions. The film was wrapped up November 4, and the day after shooting the final scene, Gable suffered a massive heart attack.

Marilyn and Miller had returned to New York on separate flights, and Marilyn was glad to hear that Gable seemed to be recovering. But she had troubles of her own to think about. On November 11, with press aide Patricia Newcomb at her side, Marilyn gave columnist Earl Wilson an exclusive: her four-year marriage to Miller was ending. (Marilyn had forgiven whatever grudge she held against Newcomb, who briefly represented her during the making of *Bus Stop* four years earlier, and hired her at the recommendation of Rupert Allan, who resigned to take another job after *The Misfits*.)

When word got out that Marilyn was again headed for divorce court, the press came running. She was prepared for their inquiries and tearfully admitted her marriage was over. But nothing could have prepared her for the news the press soon would bring her.

In the early morning hours of November 16, still awake but groggy from the pills she took to sleep, Marilyn got a call at her New York apartment from an Associated Press reporter, who told her that Gable had died. The reporter said she became hysterical and incoherent. The next morning she called the Associated Press office and said simply, "This is Marilyn. I'm sorry I couldn't talk last night. All I can say about Clark is I'm very sorry." Knowing that the media would have a field day if she showed up at Gable's funeral, she avoided the ceremony in deference to his family and pregnant wife, Kay. Shortly afterward, Marilyn heard that Kay held her partly responsible for Gable's death because of the frustrations of working with her and the long waits in her absence in the Nevada heat, which sometimes reached 110°F (43.3°C). Marilyn grew increasingly despondent and contacted her lawyer to have a new will drawn up.

Lena Pepitone, in her tell-all memoirs, said that around Christmas 1960 she found Marilyn leaning from her thirteenth-floor bedroom window, contemplating suicide. The maid said she grabbed Marilyn around the waist and pulled her inside. Biographer Summers, in interviews with Pat Newcomb, uncovered a reason for Marilyn's bleak mood beyond Gable's death and her divorce: according to Newcomb, Marilyn continued to pursue Montand. His wife, Simone, finally phoned her, "pleading with Marilyn" to "leave him alone." Montand had planned a trip to New York, and Marilyn was looking forward to being able to see him, but he canceled the trip at the last minute. Newcomb said Marilyn was "devastated."

One bright spot in her otherwise bleak Christmas that year was DiMaggio. Pepitone said he visited Marilyn

After a nervous breakdown in the desert, filming was suspended while Marilyn was treated for pill dependence. Two months later, the day after shooting wrapped, Gable suffered a massive heart attack. His death caused Marilyn extreme grief and guilt.

often, arriving around dinnertime and staying with her until morning. Also during this time, and into 1961, she would often stay overnight with the Strasbergs.

Marilyn began to have frequent meetings with attorney Aaron Frosch, who was to be executor of her will, regarding her bequests. She listed her half-sister, Berneice Baker Miracle, first in her line of heirs, followed by her secretary, May Reis. She specified a few other bequests, including an education fund for the Rostens' daughter Patricia, and arranged for the remainder of her assets, including all her personal belongings, to be given to the Strasbergs.

Marilyn and her new press agent, Pat Newcomb, grew close during their first few weeks together, as Pat recognized that Marilyn needed her as a friend as much as a press

agent. Pat became a buffer between Marilyn and the outside world; she took all of the star's calls from the media and her closest friends. She also tried to keep Marilyn in touch with reality by insisting that she return the phone calls when possible, and by taking her on excursions outside the apartment to stem her increasingly blatant pill use. Marilyn no longer cared if there were witnesses to her morning ritual of skillfully pricking the pill capsules to hasten the drugs' effect.

On Friday, January 20, 1961, accompanied by Pat and Frosch, Marilyn flew to Juarez, Mexico, to secure a speedy divorce from Miller. While John F. Kennedy took the presidential oath of office, Marilyn and her companions watched the ceremony in the lounge of a Mexican airport. She had chosen inauguration day in the hope that the press would be too occupied with the presidential proceedings to bother her about the divorce. But the press showed up in force anyway; some reporters came from as far away as Paris and Rome.

When the Mexican judge opened his office to Marilyn and the lawyers at 8 P.M., Miller's legal representative said the divorce, requested on the grounds of "incompatibility of character," was one of mutual con-

sent. Marilyn signed the papers without reading them and was back in New York by noon on Saturday. She had relinquished all rights to the Roxbury farm she had helped Miller buy, preferring to retain their New York apartment. Miller had emptied his study in the apartment while Marilyn was out, taking everything portable, except the picture of herself she had given him to hang on the wall. Marilyn also gave Miller "custody" of their dog, Hugo, saying the dog would be much happier on the farm than in her apartment. (Frank Sinatra, who resumed his courtship of Marilyn soon after her separation from Miller, gave her a white poodle to fill the void caused by her loss of Hugo. She called the dog "Maf," a name inspired by Sinatra's well-publicized mob connections.)

For the next few weeks, Pat hired John Springer to handle all of Marilyn's press relations so she could devote full time to helping Marilyn on a more personal level. The prospect of work also gave Marilyn a mental boost. Although she rarely ventured to the Actors Studio anymore, she was making plans to portray Sadie Thompson, the heroine of W. Somerset Maugham's drama *Rain*. NBC had offered her $125,000 to do a ninety-minute television special that would be taped in the spring for broadcast in autumn. Marilyn chose *Rain* after she heard about the play from Lee Strasberg, who raved about a masterful 1922 stage portrayal of Sadie by Jeanne Engels, not long before the young actress died from her heroin addiction. The only obstacle Marilyn faced was convincing NBC to name Strasberg director for the television drama.

January 31 brought the New York premiere of *The Misfits*, which was rushed into theaters as a tribute to Gable. Marilyn was escorted to the Capitol Theatre on Broadway by Montgomery Clift and Lee Strasberg. Her dissatisfaction during the making of the film was compounded by the critics' lukewarm reception; most loved Marilyn and Gable's acting, but weren't especially impressed with the story and cinematography.

In the clinic, Marilyn said she was gawked at by staff through the glass doors; this prompted her to take off her clothes after deciding that if they were "going to treat me like a nut, I'm going to act like one." She was taken to a security ward, then restrained after throwing a chair through a glass door. She told the Strasbergs in a note asking them to help her get out: "I'm sure to end up a nut if I stay in this nightmare. Please help me, Lee. This is the last place I should be.... If Dr. Kris assures you that I am all right, you can assure her I am not. I do not belong here!"

By her third day there, Marilyn was allowed to make a phone call; she immediately contacted DiMaggio. He was in Fort Lauderdale, Florida, at his Yankee Clipper Motel, and he promised to fly to New York that day

> On her notorious lateness:
>
> *I've tried to change my ways but the things that make me late are too strong and too pleasing.... I feel a queer satisfaction in punishing the people who are wanting me now.*

Audiences had expected a masterpiece created through the combined talents of America's leading playwright, actor, director, and other cast members, not to mention the blonde star of one of the most successful movies in Hollywood history, *Some Like It Hot*. But the film—which had taken forty extra days to make and was thousands of dollars over budget (*The Misfits*' $4 million cost shattered the record for black-and-white movies)—did not bring movie fans running to the theater.

Exactly one week after the premiere, Marilyn's New York therapist, Dr. Marianne Kris, convinced her patient was suicidal, talked Marilyn into entering the Payne Whitney Psychiatric Clinic to help curb her drug dependency. Marilyn walked into the clinic without hesitation on February 7, swathed in a fur coat and unaware that she was to be housed in a section for the mentally ill. After checking in as "Faye Miller," she was led through doors that banged closed and locked behind her. Realization gave way to barely contained hysteria when they took her to her room, which was sparsely furnished and had a glass door that prevented any privacy, bars on the windows, and a doorless toilet—and took away her clothing.

to secure her release. The next morning, on the arm of DiMaggio, Marilyn left the clinic through a basement passageway and was taken to Columbia-Presbyterian Hospital for admission to its Neurological Institute. For the next three weeks she rested and withdrew from pills. She never forgot her gratitude to DiMaggio. "Thank God for Joe, thank God," she later said.

A media circus surrounded Marilyn's March 5 release from the hospital, but she found relative peace back at her apartment. There Marilyn seemed to make rapid progress; the guilt she felt regarding Gable's death was eased somewhat when Gable's widow, Kay, invited Marilyn to the christening of the son Gable never saw, and Marilyn took this as a sign that Kay did not hold her responsible for her husband's death after all. Pat Newcomb then began to allow Marilyn to be interviewed, but only by reporters she determined would be sympathetic.

One such writer was Margaret Parton. Pat laid down the ground rules for Parton's mid-March interview for *Ladies Home Journal*: no questions about the past would be allowed; Marilyn was looking ahead and would be happy to talk about future plans. So Marilyn told Parton about her

*T*hree weeks after DiMaggio secured her release from a psychiatric hospital, Marilyn joined him for a short vacation in Florida.

eagerness to make *Rain* for NBC, in an attempt to show that she had control over her career. Still, the vulnerability Parton detected behind the strong facade inspired a sensitive treatment of her subject, a treatment so sensitive, in fact, that the magazine's publishers refused to print the article. One publisher, Bruce Gould, even told Parton, "If you were a man, I'd wonder what went on in that apartment." (The article finally appeared, more than sixteen years after Marilyn's death, in the February 19, 1979, issue of *Look* magazine.)

As for Marilyn's plans to make *Rain*, NBC shelved the project when she insisted upon hiring Strasberg, who had never directed a TV drama. Although she had signed a contract with the network, she refused to make the program under any other director, saying it was Strasberg's vision of Sadie that had inspired her to pursue the project in the first place.

With the NBC deal canceled, Marilyn decided to take a vacation and headed south to Florida, where DiMaggio was at the Yankees' spring-training camp. There, she visited her half-sister, Berneice Baker Miracle. (Gladys' daughter from her first marriage, Berneice was seven years older than Marilyn and living in Gainesville, not far from the Yankee camp. The two sisters had gotten in touch sometime in the late 1950s. Marilyn had been ecstatic to finally meet her sister, yet when Berneice talked about her own childhood difficulties, Marilyn responded sardonically, "At least you lived with relatives." A few weeks after Marilyn announced her divorce from Miller, Berneice visited her and was with Marilyn when she went to the Roxbury farm to collect a few items she wanted to keep.) Florida's slow pace couldn't keep Marilyn occupied for long, so after a few relaxing days spent surf fishing with DiMaggio, she returned to New York.

When she returned, Marilyn had several job offers, including some promising projects, so she decided to head to Los Angeles to check out the opportunities. Once there, however, work again took a back seat to her medical problems: doctors discovered that her fallopian tubes were blocked, and in May 1961 she checked into Cedars of Lebanon for gynecological surgery. The next month, barely recovered from her surgery on the West Coast, she entered New York's Polyclinic Hospital with an acutely inflamed gall bladder, and doctors there uncovered a sporadically bleeding uterus and an ulcerated colon. Marilyn's body was in even worse shape than her mind; despite her doctor-supervised withdrawal just weeks earlier, she continued to turn to pills and alcohol for solace.

Even before her stitches could heal, Marilyn went back to the West Coast. The few friends she still had contact with in New York had urged her to leave the City and get more involved in Hollywood, since she was spending so much time traveling there and back. She closed up her apartment for a while and headed back to Los Angeles. There, she stayed in the home of Frank Sinatra for a few weeks while he was out of town; she then returned to the Doheny Drive apartment building she'd left when she married DiMaggio. Loyal press agent Pat Newcomb followed Marilyn to Hollywood and took an apartment that was only a ten-minute drive away from her employer's home.

One day Marilyn, sounding panicked, phoned Pat to say she'd just heard from the man she believed to be her father. A card, forwarded from the New York hospital Marilyn recently left, read: "Best wishes for your early recovery. From the man you tried to see nearly ten years ago. God forgive me." When Pat arrived, Marilyn asked, "What does it mean?" then added, "It's too late." Pat decided to stay over to comfort her.

Marilyn also accelerated her sessions with Dr. Greenson, who by now was allowing the actress to meet with him at his house after he returned from his office. Marilyn saw him up to seven times a week and soon adopted his wife and children as yet another surrogate family. She became especially close to Joan Greenson, then twenty-one; Joan's brother, Danny, then twenty-four, found Marilyn far different from her image. He often spoke with her about politics.

Another person Marilyn became close to after her return to Hollywood was actress Jeanne Carmen, whom she had known since the mid-1950s from the Actors Studio in New York and who was now her neighbor at Doheny Drive. The two had much in common—Carmen also suffered from insomnia and was reliant on sleeping pills—so the two would keep each other company into the wee hours, talking and drinking.

As her reliance on narcotics increased, Marilyn began to distance herself from her closest friends, including the Strasbergs.

Both also had a great deal of time on their hands: Carmen's main employment at the time was as a trick golfer, and Marilyn did not work for the entire year of 1961.

Besides appointments with Greenson and socializing with Carmen, Marilyn spent a good deal of time with Sinatra, and by summer 1961 was even considering marriage to her favorite singer. She would go to Las Vegas to see him perform and spent a good deal of time at his Palm Springs home as well.

But from that summer on, and to a degree even in the months preceding that time, details of Marilyn's life are scarce. She no longer sought the attention of the press, whom she had courted so successfully before her move to New York to start Marilyn Monroe Productions. Pat Newcomb continued her policy of limiting press access to Marilyn unless the writer was one who would provide sympathetic coverage. As a result, in the absence of hard facts provided by interviews with Marilyn, rumors increasingly found their way into newspaper reports. Those journalists who did have access to Marilyn—mainly longtime friends such as Sidney Skolsky and James Bacon—honored her confidence until long after her death, including her talk of her involvement with President Kennedy.

Probably the best documentation of the last year or so of Marilyn's life—particularly regarding her relationship with the Kennedy clan and the resulting interest in her by powerful Mafia affiliates, who were being cracked down upon by President Kennedy and his brother Robert, the attorney general of the United States—is provided by Anthony Summers in his book *Goddess: The Secret Lives of Marilyn Monroe*. This book includes interviews with many sources who were knowledgeable about Marilyn's final months, as well as private written observations by Dr. Greenson, who died faithful to his confidential doctor-patient relationship with Marilyn. Greenson's writing paints the picture of a woman who tried to numb her intense loneliness and disappointments with promiscuity, pills, and alcohol. During her marriage to Miller and in the months after its collapse, Marilyn had many close calls with death—usually as the result of a drug overdose that was intensified by volumes of alcohol. It seems that she had no difficulty talking about and recognizing her problems, but was either unwilling or unable to alter the destructive habits that served to intensify them.

Apparently, Marilyn's 1961 Christmas was brightened by DiMaggio, who showed up with a small Christmas tree, replete with lights and trimmings, just as he did the year they met.

To keep Marilyn occupied as 1962 began, Dr. Greenson urged her to put down roots. With the help of Dr. Greenson's friend Eunice Murray, whose background included work as an interior designer, Marilyn began looking for a house to buy; by February, she was the proud owner of a modest Spanish-style home with a backyard pool on a Brentwood cul-de-sac, Fifth Helena Drive, just minutes away from Dr. Greenson and less than fifteen minutes from the Lawfords' beach house. She also retained her Doheny Drive apartment.

Photographer Eve Arnold captured a faraway Marilyn during the filming of **The Misfits**. *"Words helped to publicize her, but photographs fixed the image firmly and indelibly," Arnold wrote.*

The three-bedroom Brentwood home was long on charm but short on closet space, so piles of scripts and personal items littered most of its interior. Marilyn, notorious for spending hours on the phone at all times of the day, had two phones installed: a pink one with a listed number and a white one that was a private line. Still, in the next few months she would make many private calls from pay phones out of fear—apparently justified—that her house had been bugged since March.

At Greenson's urging, Marilyn hired Eunice as her housekeeper-companion, as Eunice had experience working with psychiatric patients. The two women eagerly set about the task of redecorating the one-story home, deciding on Mexican decor to echo its exterior. Joined by Pat Newcomb, Marilyn and Eunice flew to Mexico City in February to shop for authentic furnishings. There, Marilyn was embraced by Mexico's film community, and at a party for her she met film writer José Bolanos, with whom she had a few dates. She also visited an orphanage and filled out applications to adopt one or more of the children. She also made a generous donation to the orphanage, although the purchase of her home had left her nearly broke; she had yet to see her share of profits from her latest films.

After her return to Los Angeles, Marilyn again heard from her "father." A nurse from Palm Springs called to tell Marilyn he had suffered a heart attack and wanted to see her. After a moment of silence, she reportedly told the nurse, "Tell the gentleman I have never met him. But if he has anything specific to tell me, he can contact my lawyer. Would you like his number?" Those words echoed the message she received from this man after her attempts to contact him almost a decade earlier. Later, apparently, she felt enough sympathy to bother finding out he had recovered fully.

Besides being kept busy by remodeling chores and tending a garden at her new home, Marilyn reached an agreement with Twentieth Century-Fox over the third movie in her four-film deal with the studio. Titled *Something's Got to Give*, the film was a comedy involving a man whose wife has been lost at sea and presumed dead, only to return alive and well after

Marilyn on the set for the last time to film Something's Got to Give.

he has remarried. Marilyn wasn't enthusiastic about the Nunnally Johnson script, but the seven-year limit of her contractual obligation was almost up, and she liked the choice for her leading man, Dean Martin.

Filming of *Something's Got to Give* was set to begin in April. To prepare Marilyn for the public attention that would accompany her return to work after more than a year off, Pat Newcomb urged her to update her meager wardrobe and suggested a New York shopping spree. Marilyn returned to her East Fifty-seventh Street apartment, taking with her some upholstery fabric and a Mexican-style couch design she wanted to have made by a New York furniture maker. Being in an orderly apartment made

her all the more determined to complete work on her own home when she returned to Los Angeles later that week. But work matters were taking up much of her time for a change, so Eunice enlisted the aid of her son to ensure decorating progress while Marilyn was otherwise occupied.

In March 1962, Marilyn prepared to face the cameras again as recipient of the Golden Globe Awards' top accolade, World Film Favorite of 1961, the same honor she had been bestowed for her work in 1953, her first year as Hollywood's most popular female attraction. She also was honored that month with an invitation to see John Kennedy. Around noon on March 24, Lawford arrived to drive Marilyn to Palm Springs for a weekend with President Kennedy at the home of Bing Crosby. Lawford was kept waiting for an hour while Marilyn finished getting ready and donned a black wig to avoid public recognition.

The next month, when she was to return to Fox start filming *Something's Got to Give*, Marilyn was unable to work, reportedly suffering from a viral infection. Director George Cukor, who had worked with Marilyn on *Let's Make Love*, decided to shoot around her.

By mid-May, Marilyn had been on the set only six days in all, and Peter Levathes, the recently installed production chief for Twentieth Century-Fox, was not sympathetic to her "plight." (He was fighting to save the studio, which was sinking millions of dollars into the problem-plagued European shoot of *Cleopatra* with Elizabeth Taylor and Richard Burton.) When Marilyn did show up for work, her temperature continually hovered around 100° or 101°F (37.8° or 38.3°C), and she worked under the agreement that if it reached 103°F (39.4°C) she could go home.

Although unable to make it to the set of her new movie, Marilyn managed enough of a recovery to fly to New York on Friday, May 18, for a Madison Square Garden birthday tribute to President Kennedy that was being held the next night. Lawford had invited her to sing "Happy Birthday" to the guest of honor, and she obliged, even doling out the $1,000 admission fee for herself and an escort, her former father-in-law Isidore Miller—whom she adored and talked with on the phone at least once a week. Upon her arrival in New York, Marilyn met with Richard Meryman of *Life* magazine to plan a series of candid interviews that would take place when she returned to Los Angeles—she wanted to regain control of her image in the press. She told Meryman, "The legend may become extinct before publication day. Not the girl, the legend."

The night of the tribute, Marilyn was very nervous. She had to be sewn into her $5,000 gown (it was made to be that tight), and arrived at Madison Square Garden slightly intoxicated. In jest of her notorious lateness, Lawford repeatedly announced her appearance while she remained in the shadows and other acts performed. Finally, after announcing the "late" Marilyn Monroe, she was conspicuously nudged onto the stage.

Slowly and deliberately, her voice quite sultry from the mixture of anxiety and drugs, she began to sing her infamous (and incredibly sexy) rendition of "Happy Birthday," much to the delight of the crowd. Then, with bolstered confidence, she sang a tribute to the tune of "Thanks for the Memories" before leading the entire audience in a livelier rendition of "Happy Birthday." Kennedy quipped after her performance, "I can now retire from politics after having had 'Happy Birthday' sung to me in such a sweet, wholesome way." Marilyn attended a private party for the president afterward, then joined him at the Carlyle Hotel for a few private hours.

Following her appearance at Madison Square Garden, she and the president apparently either ceased their relationship altogether or toned it down considerably. Trysts at Lawford's Malibu beach house, in Palm Springs, and at a New York hotel had subsided following intervention by the president's younger brother Robert, supposedly at JFK's request. But his intervention apparently led to more than Marilyn's distancing from President Kennedy; Marilyn now also had set her sights on Bobby, supposedly the least philandering male in the Kennedy family. (According to Jeanne Carmen, Bobby Kennedy and Marilyn had been involved to some extent since the end of the previous summer. Carmen said she had answered the door once when Bobby visited Marilyn at her Doheny Drive apartment and that the three of them went to a nudist beach later that day.) Marilyn also kept a journal of her meetings and conversations with Bobby.

Back in Los Angeles after the gala, Marilyn placed a call to her lawyer Mickey Rudin to find out what fallout her trip might have inspired.

He recommended that she complete *Something's Got to Give*. Over the next two weeks, she managed to appear on the set six more times. Her health had obviously improved, and when questions arose over her ability to shoot a scene that required that she swim in a pool, she said she felt well enough to proceed.

On the closed set that day, May 28, were three photographers: free-lancer Lawrence Schiller and his associate William Reed Woodfield, on location for *Paris-Match*, and Jimmy Mitchell, the studio's staff photographer who was filling in for Globe Photo's photographer, who was absent due to illness. They took pictures as Marilyn got into the pool in her flesh-colored bathing suit, which she agreed to discard after the cameraman told director Cukor that it was too conspicuous. Schiller and Woodfield seized the moment, knowing its significance. They even managed to get frontal shots of Marilyn as she exited the pool.

With their rolls of film containing the first nude shots of Marilyn since her "Miss Golden Dreams" session more than thirteen years before, Schiller and Woodfield asked Marilyn if she would go through the developed photographs and approve the ones they could publish. With her promised cooperation, the enterprising photographers persuaded Globe to relinquish its rights to the film shot by Mitchell, then promised Mitchell $10,000 to allow his shots to be destroyed. The pair then contacted movie

When Marilyn took off her flesh-colored bathing suit to enhance the realism of the swimming scene in Something's Got to Give, quick-thinking photographers on the closed set took the first nude shots of the sex goddess in fourteen years.

Marilyn and the Kennedys

Marilyn Monroe was no stranger to the global political arena. Among her fans were world leaders, including President Achmed Sukarno of Indonesia, Soviet Premier Nikita Khrushchev, and Prince Rainier of Monaco. But perhaps Marilyn's most notable political affiliation was one much closer to home. While this affiliation involved the most public of officials—namely, the president of the United States, John F. Kennedy—the true details have remained closely guarded secrets. Many of those in the know, in addition to Marilyn and Kennedy, of course, are now deceased.

Some sources contend that Marilyn met Kennedy as early as 1951 at a party given by her then-agent, Charles Feldman, who frequently played host to Kennedy when the young senator visited Hollywood. The year 1951 was also about the time Marilyn befriended her idol Frank Sinatra, who was closely associated with the Kennedy clan for many years.

Marilyn acknowledged that she and Kennedy did attend the same Feldman party while she was married to Joe DiMaggio. By the end of her marriage to "The Slugger," one witness claims, Marilyn and Kennedy were more than acquaintances, frequenting various Malibu bars and motels together. That year Kennedy was hospitalized for complications from Addison's disease; on the wall of his hospital room he had hung a poster of Marilyn, affixed upside down so that her legs, set in a rather widespread stance, pointed skyward.

In 1960, Marilyn was a frequent guest at the Malibu beach house of her friends Peter and Patricia Kennedy Lawford. Another frequent Lawford guest was Senator John F. Kennedy, who often visited his sister Pat during both his campaigns for the Democratic presidential nomination and the presidency. As Marilyn's marriage to Arthur Miller steadily crumbled, she was spotted at campaign "meetings" at the beach house when Kennedy was in town.

When Kennedy was inaugurated as president of the United States, Marilyn watched the swearing-in on television from Mexico, where she had gone to obtain a speedy divorce from Miller. But she reportedly had been on hand a few months before to help Kennedy celebrate his winning the Democratic nomination; she flew to Los Angeles from New York just before starting work on The Misfits, and was seen at a party in Kennedy's honor after the nominee promised a

Coliseum crowd that they stood "...on the edge of a New Frontier...a frontier of unknown opportunities and perils." In the early months of his presidency, Marilyn also was spotted at Kennedy's New York base, the Carlyle Hotel.

Although Marilyn's affiliation with Kennedy was well concealed, word of a possible affair did get around, as is evidenced by the column Art Buchwald published the day after Kennedy was elected president:

"Let's Be Firm On Monroe Doctrine

"Who will be the next ambassador to Monroe? This is one of the many problems which President-elect Kennedy will have to work on in January. Obviously you can't leave Monroe adrift. There are too many greedy people eyeing her, and now that Ambassador Miller has left she could flounder around without any direction."

Kennedy worked out the "problem" of Marilyn by dispatching his younger brother, Robert, attorney general of the United States, as his "ambassador to Monroe" some time before the summer of 1961. As a result, Marilyn began her most tumultuous affair, one that many friends say pushed her beyond the brink barely a year later, when Robert Kennedy tried to end it.

According to at least one of Marilyn's Brentwood neighbors, Robert Kennedy was among the last people to see her alive. He was seen arriving at her home the afternoon of August 4, but his visit was brief and obviously upsetting to Marilyn, who summoned her psychiatrist after Kennedy left. It is believed that Marilyn, feeling used by the Kennedy brothers as purely "a piece of meat," refused to be set aside without a fight, however, and she reportedly threatened to expose her relationship with the two, intending to back up her claim with personal journal notations and recordings.

But before the sun rose on August 5, 1962, Marilyn lay dead on her bed, and any evidence possibly linking her to the Kennedys—including her journal—was nowhere to be found. The Kennedy brothers escaped scandal when she died (even though their enemies in organized crime knew of the affairs as well), but they could not escape doom. The next year, an assassin's bullet claimed John F. Kennedy's life. Five years later, in June 1968, Robert Kennedy, then a U.S. senator in pursuit of the presidency, met the same tragic fate while walking through the kitchen of the Ambassador Hotel in Los Angeles—the same hotel from which Marilyn's modeling career was launched in 1945, and where her aspirations of having a film career began.

Marilyn in happier times in Hollywood, 1952.

reporter Joe Hyams to handle the story, which broke two days after the shoot. When Marilyn was shown the photographs, she approved forty black-and-white and twelve color shots. Her only stipulation was that the photographers bar release of the photographs for thirty days, to allow adequate time for publications worldwide to pick them up so that she could "see all those covers with me on them and not Liz [Taylor]."

After shooting on June 1, Marilyn's thirty-sixth birthday, the crew of *Something's Got to Give* presented her with a huge birthday cake exploding with sparkling candles. Marilyn cried. (This was the last time she ever set foot on a soundstage. Later that evening, she made her last public appearance—a muscular dystrophy benefit at Chavez Ravine baseball stadium, home to the Dodgers.)

The next week, Marilyn reverted to her absenteeism. By Friday, June 8, the cast and crew heard the news: as of Thursday night, the star was off the picture; she had been fired. Costar Dean Martin's reaction was to refuse to finish the film without her. Marilyn's reaction was to seclude herself in her bedroom; she finally came out to her living room Friday evening. Waiting there was Pat Newcomb, who told her teary-eyed employer she needed a statement for the press. "Tell them I have nothing to say," Marilyn replied. "Wait! Tell them I said it's time some of the studio heads realized what they're doing. If there's anything wrong with Hollywood, it starts at the top. And something else. It seems to me it's time they stopped knocking their assets around."

Marilyn, inspired to fight in part because of Dean Martin's anger over her dismissal, put her lawyers to work to get her reinstated on the picture. After waiting about a week to see if the studio executives would reverse their decision, she left for New York. There she sat in on one of Strasberg's classes at the Actors Studio. In a show of support, the students offered her the lead role in a play they were working on. Word got out that she was preparing for a

Regarding her nude swim in Something's Got to Give:

It was just like celebrating my birthday in my birthday suit.

career switch to theater work, and her apartment was inundated with scripts. But if such a switch really was her intention, she soon abandoned that plan to return to Hollywood in late June to meet with Fox executives; she was winning the battle over *Something's Got to Give*.

Soon after her return, on June 23, Marilyn participated in an elaborate photo session for *Vogue* magazine, shot by photographer Bert Stern. She was five hours late for the first scheduled shooting at the Bel-Air Hotel. She arrived to find Stern waiting with a case of Dom Perignon, her favorite champagne. With the Everly Brothers playing in the background, Marilyn posed for a series of fashion shots, seminudes, and eventually, as she got "cheered" by the champagne, fully nude shots. Stern claimed these were the last photographs to be taken of Marilyn and published them in 1982 in his book *The Last Sitting*.

Then, on June 26, she had dinner with Robert Kennedy at the Lawford home in Palm Springs. The next day Kennedy visited Marilyn at her home, marking the last time witnesses verified her meeting with either of the Kennedy brothers.

Marilyn also began poring over the scripts that had piled up in her New York absence and found a screenplay she liked: *What a Way to Go*. This would be her next project after completing *Something's Got to Give*, for East Coast executives of Twentieth Century-Fox had overruled Levathes and the film's producer, Henry Weinstein, and reinstated Marilyn by the end of June. Production of *Something's Got to Give* would resume in September after Dean Martin completed a nightclub booking to which he was committed. Marilyn then planned a birthday party at her home for Dr. Greenson's daughter, Joan—the first and last party she would host there. She stayed close to home all summer, except for two or three trips to Sinatra's Cal-Neva Lodge (while there, the switchboard operator heard labored breathing through Marilyn's open line and summoned help, saving her from yet another overdose).

Paula Strasberg last saw Marilyn on July 30, 1962, after the actress promised to return to her New York apartment in August before resuming filming on Something's Got to Give.

Despite her victory regarding *Something's Got to Give*, Marilyn's dependence on Dr. Greenson intensified. She saw him all but seven days in July, and it appears she had plenty of reasons, in addition to the problems she had had to cope with in prior months, to need the doctor's help. On top of being fired and the battle to be rehired, Marilyn was again having to deal with rejection by a married man, this time, by all evidence, Robert Kennedy. Also that month, she and DiMaggio had a falling-out, apparently over her relationship with the Kennedys. As if this weren't enough, on July 20 she was admitted to Cedars of Lebanon Hospital—this time, several sources say, she was pregnant and either had suffered a miscarriage or sought an abortion.

Paula Strasberg flew to Los Angeles to be with Marilyn after her release from the hospital. She set about stocking her pupil's empty refrigerator and left a week later, on July 30—after Marilyn promised to return to New York and called her New York maid, telling her to prepare her apartment and informing her she would be throwing a party in September. As July turned to August, Marilyn called her old friend Henry Rosenfeld to say she would be heading to the East Coast shortly. In fact, as was Marilyn's habit her entire adult life, she stayed on the phone constantly, but instead of talking about her depression, as often had been the case of late, she was talking about the future.

After more than a year almost devoid of work, she had a string of projects to which she was committed. She made an appointment to meet with Gene Kelly on Sunday, August 5, to discuss *What a Way to Go*, in which he was to costar; she also arranged to meet with Sidney Skolsky that day, and planned a dinner date for that night with Frank Sinatra. On Monday, she pledged to meet with the film's director, Lee Thompson, before flying to New York for a meeting with composer Jule Styne to discuss her plans to make a musical version, with Sinatra, of *A Tree Grows in Brooklyn*. In the meantime, she invited makeup man Whitey Snyder and her wardrobe assistant Marjorie Plecher for drinks. They found her in "great spirits"; she "never looked better" and seemed to be pulling her life together at last.

On Friday, August 3, Marilyn's interviews earlier that summer with Richard Meryman appeared in *Life* magazine. (The sessions had been recorded on audiotape. Meryman had allowed Marilyn to review the transcripts from the previous sessions, for she said she didn't want anything in print that would hurt her stepchildren.) After months of relative silence, Marilyn once again was embracing publicity. Other interviews had been conducted that summer and new photographs were to be published soon in *Cosmopolitan* and *Vogue*, and Marilyn had been collaborating with photographer George Barris on her proposed biography. Many of Barris' photographs taken the previous month captured a slim, bikini-clad Marilyn.

George Barris took this photograph of Marilyn on July 18, 1962, two days before she was reportedly hospitalized for a miscarriage or an abortion.

Marilyn slept late that Friday, as was her custom, and prepared her own coffee and grapefruit before letting her dog, Maf, out of the guest house where he slept. Pat had planned to spend the weekend with Marilyn to help her get ready for her trip to New York, but she called to say she had bronchitis and would have to cancel. Marilyn convinced her that the best medicine would be for her to come over and lie out by the pool, and she promised to "get out the Desert-Aire lamp for you to use tonight; we'll bake those germs right out of you." Pat said she'd be over later that afternoon.

After breakfast, Marilyn visited her medical doctor, Hyman Engelberg. She asked him for a new sleeping pill prescription, complaining that her chloral hydrate tablets weren't helping, so he agreed to prescribe twenty-five tablets of Nembutal. After stopping to visit Dr. Greenson, she had the prescription filled and returned home to find Pat already there, in her bathing suit. She kept receiving calls and placed one to Norman and Hedda Rosten, who said Marilyn's voice "was high, bubbly, happy." That evening, her refrigerator already depleted despite Paula's grocery trip earlier that week, she and Pat met the Lawfords for dinner at nearby La Scala restaurant in Beverly Hills. This gathering was the last time she would ever dine out.

Friday night was a restless one for Marilyn, despite her new supply of Nembutal. By noon on Saturday, Lawrence Schiller came by to see if Marilyn had signed a contract he'd arranged with *Playboy* for publication of her nude pool pictures from *Something's*

Got to Give. The contract included plans for front and back cover photographs of Marilyn in a fur coat. She didn't tell Schiller that she already had canceled the special photo shoot a day or so earlier. He left a series of shots for her to review. When he left, she marked some of them specifically for use in *Playboy*; the marked photographs were found on Sunday in an unstamped envelope that had been shoved under Schiller's studio door. Schiller said he didn't know how the pictures got there, but speculates that Marilyn may have delivered them herself some time on Saturday.

After Schiller left, Marilyn reportedly had another visitor: Bobby Kennedy. (Even after Bobby's death six years later, Lawford repeatedly denied that his brother-in-law had been in Los Angeles that Saturday, although Kennedy was seen at the Beverly Hills Hotel on August 4 by

said, because he had a bad case of laryngitis and didn't want her to be concerned.) Dr. Greenson answered Marilyn's telephone and claimed she was out. Greenson later said Marilyn was despondent when he arrived, so he suggested she take a drive along the ocean to lift her spirits. In a conversation with Sidney Skolsky that day, Marilyn said, probably in reference to a dinner invitation extended by Lawford, "Maybe I'll go down to the beach. Everyone's going to be there." Apparently, though, she opted to stay home. Neighbors saw her around dusk playing with Maf in the backyard, tossing a ball for him to retrieve.

According to Eunice Murray, Marilyn's phone rang about every half hour that day. Marilyn also placed quite a few calls, including several to Jeanne Carmen, who said Marilyn was looking for more Nembutal and

If there's only one thing in my life I was proud of, it's that I've never been a kept woman.

both Los Angeles' former mayor, Sam Yorty, and a former chief of police, William Parker. Neighbors of Lawford contend a helicopter took someone from his beach house before midnight, and records show Lawford rented a helicopter that evening for a trip to Los Angeles International Airport— presumably with Kennedy on board.)

Apparently, Marilyn had been trying to contact Kennedy in San Francisco, where he had just arrived with his wife and four of his seven children. He had tried to end their relationship, Marilyn told friends, but she was determined to keep it alive; she even told Anne Karger the day before that she was going to marry him. Apparently, his visit that Saturday did not turn out the way she would have liked, and she placed a frantic call to Dr. Greenson.

Dr. Greenson arrived at the house late that afternoon. (Pat had left after an argument with Marilyn, telling her she would call her in the morning.) Calls had been streaming in all day to congratulate Marilyn on the *Life* interview. Callers included Marilyn's masseur, Ralph Roberts, who was on his way out to dinner; he had been asked by Rupert Allan to pass on his congratulations as well. (Allan didn't want to phone Marilyn, he

chloral hydrate. Carmen said Marilyn had been kept awake the previous night until 5:30 A.M. by an anonymous phone caller—a woman who repeatedly said, "Leave Bobby alone, you tramp."

As evening neared, Marilyn's speech became progressively slurred, according to those who spoke with her, but Eunice said she seemed to have her spirits lifted by a call just before 8 P.M. from DiMaggio's son, Joe Jr., who was now in the Armed Forces and stationed at Camp Pendleton, near San Diego. He told Marilyn he had broken his engagement. "He sounded so relieved, I'm happy for him," Marilyn said to Eunice before telling her housekeeper-companion, who was spending the night at Greenson's request, "Goodnight, honey." Eunice then heard Marilyn's record player come on; she was listening to Frank Sinatra.

Author Fred Guiles offers the following version of what he believed happened next: "Between 10 and 11 that evening, panic must have aroused Marilyn from the stupor that always preceded an overdose. If she attempted to phone Pat Newcomb or one of her doctors, she was unsuccessful in reaching them. But she did get through to the two men [Lawford and Robert Kennedy] who had invited her out that evening, and she told one of the men that she had just taken the last of her Nembutals and she was about to slip over the line. One of them attempted to phone Mickey Rudin, Marilyn's Hollywood attorney, but he was out for the evening. Why such indirect means of summoning help were chosen will never be known. Oddly enough, it occurred to no one who was aware of what was happening to inform the police....

"In a last conscious attempt, Marilyn dialed yet another number. Ralph Roberts' answering service reported to him that he had received a call from a woman who sounded fuzzy-voiced and troubled, but had left no name or number. In all likelihood, Marilyn's last contact with a human being was the voice of an operator informing her that Mr. Roberts was out for the evening." Marilyn probably took her last breath sometime before midnight, August 4.

The biggest mystery of Marilyn's death is not necessarily whether she had intended to kill herself by overdose. Most believe her death to be accidental; she did, after all, reach out for help. It is curious that she didn't seek help from Eunice, who was just a few steps away, when her other attempts failed. Perhaps she thought those she contacted—particularly Lawford—would arrive in time for yet another rescue. Official reports show that her doctors had found her clutching a phone in her hand, most probably her private line.

Eunice told reporters the next morning that she awoke at about 3 A.M. with an "uneasy feeling" and went to Marilyn's bedroom door to rouse her. When she got no response, she said she went outside and looked into the bedroom through the closed French windows to see Marilyn outstretched on the bed and looking "peculiar." Eunice said she then called Dr. Greenson, who quickly arrived and broke into Marilyn's room through the window. Finding Marilyn dead and in an early stage of rigor mortis, he phoned Dr. Engelberg. Engelberg confirmed Marilyn's death when he arrived at around 3:30 A.M., Eunice said, and the police were called about a half hour later. Eunice would continually alter this story somewhat as time progressed.

The first officers to arrive on the scene—two radio patrolmen and Sergeant Jack Clemmons—found it odd to see Eunice straightening up the house and doing laundry. After about an hour

the three officers were joined by Detective Sergeant R.E. Byron. By then Clemmons had placed a call to his friend and fellow officer Jim Dougherty. "An OD it looks like," Clemmons said. "I knew you'd want to know." The news came as no great shock to Marilyn's first husband, who said to his wife, "Say a prayer for Norma Jeane. She's dead."

Pat Newcomb told police she was home when Mickey Rudin called her at about 4 A.M. to tell her that Marilyn was dead. Pat hurriedly dressed and drove to Marilyn's house, then reportedly became hysterical upon seeing her friend and employer. Pat said she blamed herself for not spending the night as they had planned. When she left the house after about an hour, the yard was already swarming with photographers. "Keep shooting, vultures!" she yelled as she left, just before county detectives officially

A coroner's seal was affixed on the front door of Marilyn's Brentwood house to bar anyone from entering, but the scene of her death apparently was tampered with just the same, adding to the mystery surrounding the exact circumstances of her death.

Marilyn's death was front-page news around the world, as evidenced by this montage of Italian newspapers from the day after her death.

sealed Marilyn's house. Among the reporters already on the scene by dawn were James Bacon and Joe Hyams. Joe Ramirez, a *City News* agency reporter with contacts at the coroner's office, was the first journalist to report her death; he had the story on the wires by about 5 A.M. For the next eighteen hours, Pat fielded close to 250 calls from around the world.

Marilyn's former business agent Inez Melson—legal custodian of Marilyn's mother, Gladys—reached the house before the coroner's arrival. She was allowed into the bedroom. "There were pill bottles, some empty, some full, on the nightstand and dresser," she said. "I walked into the bathroom and saw the cabinet's shelves crowded with Marilyn's allergy pills, tranquilizers, and sleeping tablets. I had an impulse to run through those two rooms, snatching up the bottles and hiding them in my bag, but I knew that was impossible." One of the empty bottles had been filled with twenty-five capsules of Nembutal just thirty or so hours earlier. Melson says that when she returned the next day and saw the pill bottles undisturbed, she flushed the remaining pills and threw away the containers.

The cause of Marilyn's death seemed obvious: she had taken a lethal dose of sleeping pills. Her body was carted away to the Westwood Village Mortuary, then on to the county morgue. But the ensuing autopsy there served to raise even more questions than it answered.

The medical autopsy was performed by Dr. Thomas Noguchi, then deputy medical examiner. The chief coroner had left a note on Noguchi's desk assigning him the Monroe case; observing the procedure for the district attorney's office was John Miner. Noguchi found Marilyn's 117-pound (53kg) body to have been in good condition—"well-developed, well-nourished." His examination of her stomach revealed congestion and a hemorrhaging of the stomach lining, but he found no trace of any pills or capsules. The cause of death would not be determined surgically; that was up to the toxicology lab.

Head Toxicologist Ralph Abernethy found that Marilyn had ingested around ten times the normal dose of Nembutal and about twenty times the usual dosage of chloral hydrate—the quantity of each drug by itself enough to kill a person. No alcohol was found in her bloodstream, indicating she'd had nothing alcoholic to drink for many hours before her death.

One mystery that remains is how Marilyn took the pills. The water in her bathroom had been cut off because of renovation work, and no drinking glass was found in the bedroom. Some speculate she may have broken open the capsules and drank the contents; another theory is that she administered the drugs rectally, via an enema. Unfortunately, these questions may never be answered, because the coroner's office failed to investigate how the drugs were administered, and tissue samples that could provide the answers were inexplicably destroyed.

In the absence of any cut-and-dried death scenario, speculation still abounds as to how and when she died, whether her death was intentional suicide or an accidental overdose, or whether it was actually murder. More questions arise from the behavior of investigators, which included the seizure and the apparent altering of Marilyn's phone records, reportedly by the FBI. Questions also abound as to whether someone actually did arrive in time to help Marilyn.

James Hall, in a May 1986 article for *Hustler* magazine, claims he was an ambulance driver in August 1962 for Schaefer Ambulance service and that his unit answered a call from Marilyn's house just after midnight on the morning of August 5. He claimed Marilyn was unconscious but alive when the ambulance arrived. Walt Schaefer, head of the ambulance company, confirmed in interviews with Anthony Summers that a unit had been called to her house that night, but added that she was taken to Santa Monica Hospital, where she died. He said the ambulance bill was later paid by Marilyn's estate.

Who called the ambulance? Was someone at Marilyn's home as her life slipped away? If she did die at the hospital, how did her body end up on her bed? Natalie Jacobs, the wife of press-agency owner Arthur Jacobs, said her husband was interrupted by a call from Pat Newcomb during a Henry Mancini concert, saying Marilyn had died, and that he arrived at Marilyn's at around 11:30 Saturday night. Another person placed at Marilyn's home the night she died was Peter Lawford.

Private investigator Fred Otash said he was awakened that Saturday night by a call from Lawford, who said he had "a big problem" and needed to see Otash right away. Lawford arrived at Otash's door in the early morning hours of August 5, looking "half-cocked or half-doped" and immediately said, "Marilyn's dead." He told Otash he already had been to her house to "clean up," to search for any documents or recordings that would link Marilyn to the Kennedy brothers, but he was afraid he might have missed something. Otash immediately sent to her house an associate who had installed eavesdropping devices there months earlier, and some personal documents were removed. (Otash said the bugging was ordered by Mafia associates interested in Marilyn's relationship with the Kennedys, who had been cracking down on mob activities. He said tapes made at Marilyn's home during the months hence left no doubt that she and at least President Kennedy were "having a sexual relationship.")

Aside from the conflicting testimony, confusing scenarios, and numerous questions about what transpired that night—most of which can never be resolved—the only indisputable fact was the tragic outcome: Marilyn Monroe was dead at the age of thirty-six.

Marilyn's body, Coroner's Case No. 81128, lay unclaimed for hours on a cold slab at the Los Angeles County Morgue. "Marilyn was dead and there seemed to be no one to claim her," Fred Guiles wrote. "Her life had ended as it had begun."

But Marilyn's attorneys, Aaron Frosch of New York, executor of her estate, and Mickey Rudin were already in touch with Berneice Miracle, Marilyn's half-sister. Berneice also spoke with DiMaggio by phone; he had flown to Los Angeles as soon as he heard the news Sunday morning, and he agreed to handle all the funeral arrangements until Berneice could arrive from Florida on Monday.

Rudin contacted makeup man Whitey Snyder on Monday, August 6, in honor of Marilyn's expressed wish that no one but Snyder was to touch

Marilyn's half-sister, Berneice Miracle (left), with Inez Melson, conservator of Marilyn's mother's estate, at Westwood Village Mortuary in West Los Angeles.

her. When Snyder arrived at the mortuary, he carried in his pocket a money clip Marilyn had given him years earlier that was inscribed "To Whitey. While I'm still warm. Marilyn." He also carried to the preparation room a fifth of gin that he'd picked up at the liquor store to help him through his task. "I decided I couldn't go through it sober," he said. Costumer Marjorie Plecher was asked to dress Marilyn for the last time, choosing Marilyn's favorite dress, a green Pucci design; Agnes Flanagan, one of Marilyn's favorite hair stylists, agreed to do her hair, finally settling on a pageboy-style wig Marilyn had worn in *The Misfits*. "There was an eerie sense of perverse remembered ritual about the three members of Marilyn's staff getting her ready for her final appearance," Guiles wrote.

Only twenty-five guests were invited to attend Marilyn's funeral on August 8, among them DiMaggio and his son, the Strasbergs, the Greenson family, Anne and Mary Karger, and two of Marilyn's former foster parents. Arthur Miller, who was remarried (to photographer Inge Morath, whom he had met on the set of *The Misfits*) did not attend because, he said, "she's not really there anymore." Conspicuously omitted from the guest list were the Lawfords, Sinatra, and other Hollywood "friends" from her later years. DiMaggio said in defense of omitting them from the list, "But for those friends she'd still be alive." These people showed up outside the funeral nonetheless and were denied admission.

DiMaggio spent a night of mourning before the open-casket funeral with Marilyn's body at the mortuary; she was buried with the roses he placed in her hands. At the service at the new Westwood Village Mortuary Chapel, Lutheran minister A.J. Soldan read the Twenty-third Psalm and parts of the fourteenth chapter of the Book of John and the Forty-sixth and One-hundred-thirty-ninth Psalms. Lee Strasberg delivered the eulogy, and the chapel was filled with the soft strains of Judy Garland's "Over the Rainbow." After the service, DiMaggio said good-bye to his former wife with a final "I love you" and a kiss. Then Marilyn was taken in her bronze casket to a crypt at Westwood Memorial cemetery.

DiMaggio arranged for a pair of red roses to be delivered to Marilyn's vault "twice a week—forever." Twenty years later, in September 1982, he suddenly decided that "forever" was over: he canceled the order. But Robert Slatzer picked up where DiMaggio left off; white roses now fill the black vase at her crypt, and Slatzer has arranged to keep the flowers coming long after his death.

The stark plaque that marks Marilyn's final resting place—"Marilyn Monroe 1926–1962"—makes no mention of the real Norma Jeane that always lived just beneath the skin of Marilyn the legend. Perhaps only in death could Marilyn give Norma Jeane the peace and permanence she had so long sought.

Marilyn's crypt was adorned with red roses sent by DiMaggio for twenty years after her death.

A Eulogy
for Marilyn

The man that Marilyn had relied on most for help in

becoming a serious, respected actress, Lee Strasberg, was

on hand to help lay his tormented pupil to rest on August 8,

1962. He delivered the following eulogy at her funeral:

"Despite the heights and brilliance she attained on the screen,

she was planning the future: she was looking forward to participat-

ing in the many exciting things which she planned. In her eyes and in

mine, her career was just beginning.

"The dream of her talent, which she had nurtured as a child,

was not a mirage. When she first came to me I was amazed at the

startling sensitivity which she possessed and which had remained

fresh and undimmed, struggling to express itself despite the life to

which she had been subjected. Others were as physically beautiful

as she was, but there was obviously something more in her, some-

thing that people saw and recognized in her performances and with

which they identified. She had a luminous quality—a combination of

wistfulness, radiance, yearning—that set her apart and yet made everyone wish to be a part of it, to

share in the childish naiveté which was at once so shy and yet so vibrant. This quality was even

more evident when she was on the stage.

"I am truly sorry that the public who loved her did not have the opportunity to see her as we

did, in many of the roles that foreshadowed what she would have become. Without a doubt she would

have been one of the really great actresses of the stage."

The happy,
alluring face Marilyn
put on for her adoring
public belied deep
and private frustrations
in both her personal
life and career.

The Legend Survives

It scares me. All those people [fans]

I don't know, sometimes there're so emotional.

I mean, if they love you that much

without knowing you, they can also

hate you in the same way.

arilyn's death had profound, far-reaching effects. In the weeks following her death, the suicide rate in Los Angeles County alone jumped 40 percent. Young girls mourning their screen idol killed themselves by taking lethal doses of sleeping pills.

Among the suicide attempts prompted by Marilyn's death were at least two by her mother, Gladys, still a patient at Rockhaven Sanitarium. Months later, in 1963, Gladys climbed down a rope of knotted sheets and found her way to a church in the San Fernando Valley. There she told the minister, J. Brian, "Marilyn, she has left. They told me about it after it happened. People ought to know that I never did want her to become an actress in the first place. Her career never did her any good."

(Gladys was transported back to Rockhaven, but three years later she left for good. She contacted her daughter Berneice, who sent her a one-way ticket to Florida and admitted her to another hospital. Berneice became her legal guardian in 1967. Gladys lived to marry again and was finally considered well enough to live out the rest of her life outside a mental institution. She died of heart failure in 1984.)

Little physical evidence outside of photographs and films remains of Marilyn's short life. The Brentwood home was bought at auction by a doctor, Gilbert Nunez. Her white poodle, Maf, found a new home with Frank Sinatra's secretary, Gloria Lovell. Her Los Angeles bank account held a paltry $5,000, and her New York bank account was overdrawn. The Strasbergs inherited the bulk of her estate. Paula died in 1966. Lee remarried; after his death in 1982 his widow, actress Anna Mizrahi, took over and franchised the licensing of Monroe objects.

Marilyn's mother, Gladys, shown here on July 5, 1963, as she was returned to the Glendale, California, sanitarium from which she had escaped the day before. She eventually lived outside the institution.

Marilyn memorabilia is a multimillion-dollar business, and even Madonna has profited from copying Marilyn's look and style ("I can feel the spirit of Marilyn Monroe in me," Madonna once said).

Marilyn memorabilia is a multimillion-dollar business, with objects ranging from posters and greeting cards to dolls and dishes. And at least one group of fans, the Marilyn Monroe International Fan Club based in Long Beach, California, has been attempting for years to make the star's face even more prevalent by putting it on a postage stamp.

Even Marilyn, with her keen awareness of the power of popularity, probably would be amazed by the effects of her death and especially by the status she maintains even today, decades after her death. She is one of the most written about, most mimicked, and most loved persons in history. She is cited as a primary inspiration by modern performers— singers Madonna and Deborah Harry are two of the most successful.

Artists and filmmakers have used Marilyn's image as an icon for pop culture. Even in death she contributed to Andy Warhol's reign as king of Pop Art with his "Marilyn" silk-screen overpainting. "It was all so simple—quick and chancy," Warhol said. "I was thrilled by it. My first experiment with screens were heads of Troy Donahue and Warren Beatty, and when Marilyn happened to die that month, I got the idea to make a screen of her beautiful face—the first Marilyn."

Photographs have been altered to make Marilyn the Statue of Liberty; the object of Vincent van Gogh's obsession, holding his severed ear; and a lone female among a choir of

News of Marilyn's death inspired Pop artist Andy Warhol to produce the first silkscreen of her face, then to expand the concept into his series of colorful portraits.

singing sailors. But such camp would probably please Marilyn, for camp was a niche at which she was highly adept. Songs have been written about her, as well as dozens—maybe hundreds—of books.

During her lifetime, Marilyn had scores of imitators, none of whom could come close to capturing the magic she conveyed. Jayne Mansfield tried, as did other stars bleached blonde by their studios in hopes of displacing the queen of Hollywood: Carroll Baker, Mamie Van Doren, Joi Lansing, Beverly Michaels, Barbara Nichols, Sheree North—the list is practically endless. Many had the necessary beauty, but none possessed the mysterious spark. Even those directors and producers who found Marilyn to be a thorn in their side on the set later admitted that she had a special quality and luminosity that can't be taught or tamed.

Look-alike mannequins in Monroe costumes face New York's Fifth Avenue from the windows of the Piaget Building in autumn 1992.

The anniversaries of Marilyn's birth and death are marked around the world by fans who know of her, and by the curious, who want to know of her. Look-alike contests are so commonplace that many impersonators make a fair living from the prizes offered. Actresses turn out in droves for auditions to portray Marilyn in films and on television. Even as what would have been her sixty-fifth birthday came and went, one television network was casting for yet another show depicting her struggles as Norma Jeane before forever adopting the name Marilyn—a name that she admitted she disliked, saying she wished she had insisted on being called Jean Monroe. "But," as she said in a 1952 interview, "I guess it's too late to do anything about it now."

Appendices

The Films of Marilyn Monroe

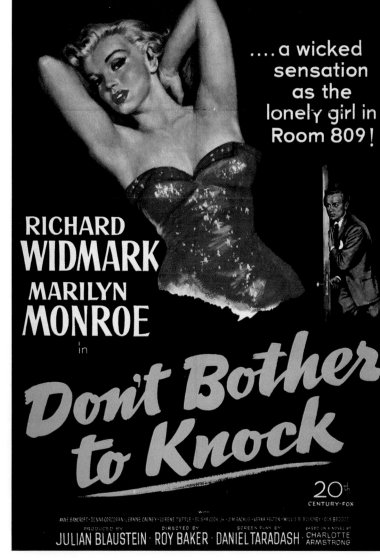

Film	Release Date
O. Henry's Full House	1952
Niagara	1953
Gentlemen Prefer Blondes	1953
How to Marry a Millionaire	1953
River of No Return	1954
There's No Business Like Show Business	1954
The Seven Year Itch	1955
Bus Stop	1956
The Prince and the Showgirl	1957
Some Like It Hot	1959
Let's Make Love	1960
The Misfits	1961

Bibliography

Arnold, Eve. *Marilyn Monroe: An Appreciation*. New York: Alfred A. Knopf, Inc., 1987.

Guiles, Fred Lawrence. *Norma Jean: The Life of Marilyn Monroe*. Hyattstown, N.J.: McGraw-Hill Book Company, 1969.

McCann, Graham. *Marilyn Monroe*. New Brunswick, N.J.: Rutgers University Press, 1988.

Miller, Morton. "My Moments With Marilyn." *Esquire* (June 1989): 161–164.

Monroe, Marilyn. *My Story*. Detroit, Mich.: Stein and Day, 1974.

Riese, Randall, and Neal Hichens. *The Unabridged Marilyn: Her Life From A to Z*. New York: Congdon & Weed, 1987.

Shaw, Sam, and Norman Rosten. *Marilyn Among Friends*. New York: Henry Holt & Company, 1987.

Spada, James. "The Man Who Kept Marilyn's Secrets." *Vanity Fair* (May 1991): 157–162.

Steinem, Gloria. *Marilyn*. New York: Henry Holt & Company, 1986.

Summers, Anthony. *Goddess: The Secret Lives of Marilyn Monroe*. New York: Macmillan Publishing Company, 1985.

Index

Photography Credits